The cat-care handbook

The cat-care handbook

Clare Gibson

ISLAND BOOKS

This edition published in 2003 by
S. WEBB & Son (Distributors) LTD
Telford Place, Pentraeth Road,
Menai Bridge,
Isle of Anglesey, LL59 5RW

© 2003 D&S Books Ltd

D&S Books Ltd
Kerswell,
Parkham Ash, Bideford
Devon, England
EX39 5PR

e-mail us at:-
enquiries@dsbooks.fsnet.co.uk

This edition printed 2003

ISBN 1-856057-58-5

Creative Director: Sarah King
Editor: Judith Millidge
Project editor: Anna Southgate
Photographer: Paul Forrester
Designer: Axis Design Editions

Printed in Singapore

This book was set in Futura BT, Akzidenz Grotesk & GillSans

1 3 5 7 9 10 8 6 4 2

Contents

FELINE EYES HAVE PROMPTED MANY SUPERSTITIONS.

gratitude to the cat who kept the baby Jesus warm in his manger in Bethlehem. Echoing the tale of Dick Whittington, sometime mayor of London, certain Western European folk beliefs furthermore tell of cats (called *matagots* in southern France) that typically repay their owners' kindness with riches and other life-transforming rewards.

Such positive feline associations are sadly rare in Christianity, however, whose influence decimated the feline population of Europe (with the result that, as some social historians believe, rats flourished, enabling the bubonic plague, or Black Death, to sweep in deadly swathes across Europe). Long before they were converted to Christianity, the Celts, who told of terrible giant cats that did battle with their heroes, sacrificed their 'evil' feline representatives on earth in religious rites. Whether or not such old beliefs

simply persisted or newer anti-feline sentiments replaced them, from medieval times until the last of the vicious witch hunts that infected Europe until the age of Enlightenment, the Roman Catholic Church branded cats – especially black ones – the servants of Satan. They were regarded as the nocturnal (in itself considered suspicious, along with their eerily glowing eyes) 'familiars', or demonic helpers, of witches, who were, of course, in league with the devil. Part of the cat's association with witchcraft dates back to its link with the Roman goddess Diana, whom the Church accused medieval 'witches' of invoking in their sinister satanic rituals, as well as with Hekate, or Hecate, the fearsome Graeco-Roman goddess of the underworld who transformed the maiden Galinthias into a cat to serve as her priestess. A more prosaic explanation, however, is that the lonely old women who were accused of witchcraft were often outcasts who had only their pet cats for companionship.

A vital justification of the Church's attempt to stamp out any beliefs that it regarded as being heretical was the damning 'evidence' that those accused of being heretics carried out satanic rites in which the devil was worshipped in the form of a black cat. (The satanic symbolism of

the black cat was potent: the epidemic of Sydenham's chorea, or St Vitus's dance, that raged through what is now the French town of Metz in 1344 was said to have been caused by Satan in the form of a black cat, and for centuries thereafter cats were publicly burned in the spirit of commemorative revenge.) And when Europe's mass 'heresies' had been all but eradicated, the Church turned to smaller fry – 'witches' and their 'familiars'. In his instructions to the Inquisition, for example, Pope Innocent VIII (who reigned from 1484 to 1492) ordering the hunting-down of cat-idolaters.

In England, the ascent to the throne of James VI of Scotland as James I in 1603 heralded a virulent period of anti-witch hysteria, fuelled by the new king's authorship of a treatise on witchcraft, *Daemologie* (1597), and compounded by the Witchcraft Act of 1604. The salacious transcriptions of the trials of the unfortunates accused of witchcraft, such as Agnes and Joan Waterhouse and Elizabeth Francis at Chelmsford in 1566, are strewn with references to feline familiars, in this case 'Sathan' (unusually, a white-spotted cat, albeit supposedly a blood-sucking one), whom Agnes Waterhouse, it was said, once 'toke . . . in her lap and put hym in the wood before her door, and wylled him to kyll three of the Father

Kersyes hogges'. Agnes Waterhouse was hanged, and if Sathan was captured, it is likely that he suffered an agonising death. (Perhaps cats have ancestral memories of those terrible times, and maybe it is no quirk of nature that domestic cats can adapt to the feral lifestyle so readily.)

Vestiges of such irrational anti-feline prejudices survived long after the last 'witch' swung from the gibbet. Dead cats were often laid in the foundations of buildings to ward off evil (or rodents: Bohemian farmers believed, for instance, that burying a cat in a field would protect their crops from mice). A black cat crossing one's path was said by some to be a harbinger of bad luck (although British superstition stipulates the reverse), while spiteful women were sometimes described as being 'catty'. And if that wasn't enough, cats are said to cause bad weather, too.

BLACK CATS SIGNIFY BOTH GOOD AND BAD LUCK.

17

Raining cats and dogs

King James's interest in witchcraft had been kindled in 1590 by the trial of Dr John Fian, who was accused of having used sorcery to try to kill the king himself as he returned from Denmark to Scotland by sea. It was alleged that Fian and his coven had thrown cats into the sea in a murderous attempt to whip up a ship-wrecking storm, an expedient that would not have sounded so ridiculous to the sixteenth-century ear as it does to us today. Indeed, nautical lore holds that throwing the ship's cat overboard will result in a storm (but presumably disposing of the ship's vermin-killer-in-chief should only be done in the most desperate of circumstances), while trapping one in a barrel can produce a contrary wind. (Conversely, Japanese sailors believe that the tortoiseshell Mi-Ke cats that they welcome aboard have the power to repel storm devils.)

Folk belief has long credited felines and canines with the ability to influence the weather – hence the expression 'raining cats and dogs', with cats denoting torrential rain and dogs storm winds – an attribution that probably stems in part from the powers and characteristics of the Norse gods and their attendant creatures and in part to both animals' acute sensitivity to changes in the weather and the cat's to water in particular. A further traditional belief is that cats can act as feline weather-forecasters if you know how to read the signs, as Jonathan Swift, the author of *Gulliver's Travels* (1726), explained in verse:

Careful observers may foretell the hour
(By sure prognostics) when to dread a shower;
While rain depends, the pensive cat gives o'er
Her frolics, and pursues her tail no more.

Swift's reference to tail-pursuing echoes the nautical expression 'the cat has a gale of wind in her tail', describing a cat's agitation when it senses a stiff following wind, as well as the belief that rain is imminent when a cat settles down to enjoy a thorough ear-washing session.

BAD WEATHER

WHILE THE CAT IS ASSOCIATED WITH RAIN, STORM WINDS ARE THE DOG'S PROVINCE.

CASPAR, THE CROSSPED

MY OWN CATS: CASPAR, THE DARK-SILVER TABBY, AND MELCHIOR, THE LIGHT-SILVER SOMALI.

Introducing Caspar and Melchior

Despite the devoted attention that they pay to ear-washing, sadly neither of our two cats seem to possess the power – or, perhaps, the inclination – to save us the bother of watering the garden on a sultry summer's night. Caspar and Melchior will be putting in an occasional appearance in the pages of this book to illustrate some of the choices and problems – as well as the pleasures – that all cat-owners inevitably face. I hope that sharing our experience of their habits and idiosyncrasies, as well as of the ailments that have afflicted them during the past twelve years and the care strategies that we have used (some successful, others less so), will prove useful to you.

Caspar and Melchior have been constant – if often mutually intolerant – companions for most of their lives. Born a couple of weeks apart at the same cat-rescue sanctuary, Caspar is a dark-silver tabby (a crosspedigree, or 'crossped' for short, a name that describes both his parentage and sometimes also his mood when food doesn't materialise fast enough), while Melchior is a light-silver Somali, although, having no pedigree certificate, I cannot vouch for the purity of his lineage. Neither cat's parentage matters to us, but pedigree is of vital

importance to many cat-owners. (And 'owner' is not really an accurate description of those who live with cats, most of whom know that if anyone can be said to be 'owned' in a human–feline relationship, it is the human. The intractability of the cat is reflected in British law, which holds that because it is a wild animal that cannot be controlled, its 'owner' cannot be held responsible for its actions, in contrast to a dog, whose owner must both licence it and be prepared to be held to account for any damage or nuisance that it causes.)

21

Of crosspeds and purebreds

As we have seen, although European domestic cats were largely left to fend for themselves and to breed unchecked, their Oriental cousins often led a more sheltered existence and were subjected to controlled breeding to ensure that the characteristics that were so prized in their particular breed remained untainted. Thus while medieval depictions of European cats reveal how the leggy elegance of their Egyptian ancestors gradually gave way to stocky sturdiness (probably as a result of interbreeding with the European wildcat, *Felis sylvestris*), the physical characteristics of Orientals have remained remarkably unchanged throughout the course of history.

The predominant type of European domestic cat is the shorthair, of which the tabby is one of the most common examples. The name 'tabby' is ultimately derived from the al-'attabiya area of Baghdad, in Iraq, where the watered silk that resembles the blotched pattern of some tabbies' coats was first manufactured, another characteristic pattern being Caspar's striped, or

THE APPEARANCE OF MANY ORIENTAL CATS HAS CHANGED LITTLE OVER THE CENTURIES.

mackerel, coat configuration. Longhaired cats are not indigenous to Europe, but were introduced from the East by smitten European travellers during the sixteenth century, the first breed to arrive being the Angora, from Turkey – the French statesman Cardinal Richelieu (1585–1642) owned one, which he rather provocatively, especially in view of his rank in the Catholic Church, named Lucifer – followed by the Persian, from Iran. Such exotic Eastern felines were initially 'luxury' pets, feline status symbols that belonged exclusively to the most

privileged members of society, a situation that would, however, change during the nineteenth century with the advent of the 'cat fancier', of whom Harrison Weir was the most notable. Although dog shows had become commonplace during the nineteenth century, no such dedicated arena existed in which to admire the feline's inimitable qualities, a deficiency that the cat-loving Weir decided to remedy 'so that different breeds, colours, markings, etc, might be more carefully attended to, and the domestic cat sitting in front of the fire would then possess

THE TYPICAL TABBY COAT PATTERN IS EITHER BLOTCHED OR STRIPED.

23

introduction

a beauty and an attractiveness to its owner unobserved and unknown because uncultivated heretofore'. As a result of Weir's energy and determination, the first formal cat show, at which 160 felines were exhibited in 25 classes, was held in London's Crystal Palace in 1871. A resounding success with its Victorian visitors, the show was responsible for launching the phenomenon of the 'cat fancy', and with it a

SIAMESE CAT

CAT SHOWS ARE TODAY AMONG THE HIGHLIGHTS OF THE '

plethora of new breeds.

Whereas cats once exhibited only a handful of coat colours, today they are resplendent in more than fifty, while their eye colouring ranges from yellow to blue to green, and, in the case of the odd-eyed white Persian, one even being blue and the other orange. The coat can be either the tabby's agouti (striped or ticked with different-coloured bands along the length of each hair), self-coloured (plain), two-toned (as seen in smoke, shell, shaded or tortoiseshell fur) or pointed (with the extremities displaying a contrasting shade to the body), as well as shorthaired, semi-longhaired or longhaired, while the somewhat controversial Sphynx has no hair at all. Build and character vary widely between the breeds, too, from the lithe, highly sociable Siamese, to the bushy-tailed, ultra-laid-back Ragdoll.

SPHYNX CAT

YEAR.

The number of cat breeds continues to grow, and to describe them all would require another book. To take just one example, the Somali breed evolved about twenty years ago in North America from longhaired mutations born to shorthaired Abyssinians. Defying the sceptics, some romantics believe that Abyssinians (and thus also Somalis) originated in Ethiopia, to the south-east of Egypt, and that because they so closely resemble the cats of ancient Egyptian art they are descended from Bast's sacred cats (a theory that, I suspect, our Somali, Melchior, would promote if he thought that it would win him extra food and cosseting).

Be they pedigrees or moggies, Somalis or crosspeds, however, every cat, to cannibalise the words of the poet Graham R Tomson, are sphinxes of our quiet hearths, whose lore is that of the ancient Egyptian gods Ra and Rameses. I hope that this book will answer any questions that you may have about how to understand and care for your own house sphinx.

OWNING A CAT OR TWO WILL PROVIDE YOU WITH A SOURC

ENTERTAINMENT.

27

The feline world

Appearances can be deceptive: however innocent and harmless your cat may appear, its genetic software has programmed it to be a hunter of the kind who shows no mercy and takes no prisoners. Its ancestors may have found it convenient to trade their wild existence for the relative ease of a domesticated lifestyle, but make no mistake: your cat will revert to its roots in an instant if its hunting instinct is aroused or its home conditions no longer suit it. Even the most indolent of house cats remains essentially wild, with a body and mentality that evolution has honed to focus above all on the pursuit and capture of prey.

CATS START TO LEARN AND PRACTISE THEIR HUNTING SKILLS IN KITTENHOOD.

HOWEVER DOMESTICATED THEY MAY APPEAR, ALL CATS ARE WILDCATS BY NATURE.

While domestication has to some extent altered the way in which the cat views its world (in the human–feline household regarding its owners as having assumed its mother's role, for example), scratch the surface of the feline psyche and evidence of its deeply embedded ancestral inheritance immediately becomes apparent. As the zoologist Desmond Morris puts it in his book *Catwatching* (1992), 'As it crosses the threshold [to go outside] the cat becomes transformed. The kitten-of-man brain is switched off and the wild-cat brain is clicked on'. Do not try to reprogramme your house feline's wildcat brain – not only will you be fighting a losing battle, but you will at best only succeed in confusing your cat, resulting in all sorts of behavioural problems, and, in the worst-case scenario, even forcing it to leave home to try its luck in more cat-congenial surroundings. And if you cannot stomach the thought of disposing of the corpses of small creatures that may occasionally materialise on your kitchen floor – the natural conclusion of the feline hunting instinct – think twice before adopting a cat.

31

WHEN A DOMESTIC CAT SIGHTS A POTENTIAL MEAL, ITS KILLER INSTINCTS COME TO THE FORE.

Rather than making the mistake of crediting your cat with human emotions and motivations, or trying to force it to behave in a way that is alien to it, try to understand what makes it tick. Gaining an appreciation of feline physiology and psychology, as outlined in the following pages, will enrich both of your lives and will strengthen the bond between you and your cat.

A hunter's build

Evolution having fine-tuned every fibre, nerve and cell of the feline body many millennia ago, the domestic cat of the twenty-first century closely resembles its wildcat ancestors in both build and mentality. Like every other species – *Homo sapiens* included – the cat's ultimate *raison d'être* is the constant search for, and acquisition of, food, a mission for which nature has equipped it superbly.

Reflecting its wildcat pedigree, the cat is a predatory carnivore whose natural diet consists exclusively of small mammals, typically rodents, such as mice and rats, that are small enough for it to pounce on and dispatch without incurring serious injury. Contrary to the popular view of cats as bird-killers, although cats will often stalk birds, the avian talent for vertical take-off make them harder to catch than ground-hugging rodents.

CATS ON THE PROWL ARE CONSTANTLY ON THE ALERT FOR PREY.

Similarly, despite the specialised piscine-preying prowess of the wild fishing cat of southern Asia, fish do not form part of the cat's staple diet.) And because rodents are largely nocturnal, cats prowl our gardens at night in search of easy pickings, much as their ancestors would have stalked the dusty terrain of Egypt. Nor is its night vision the only example of the physical traits that make it a hunting specialist, for from the tips of its whiskers to the end of its tail the cat is a hunting machine *par excellence*.

EVEN RELAXED CATS REMAIN ALERT.

Among the cat's most celebrated attributes are its remarkable agility and innate talent for acrobatics – which must surely make it the envy of any circus entertainer – both of which enable it to get into, and out of, the tightest and most awkward of spots.

FELINE WHISKERS ARE VITAL SENSORY TOOLS.

CATS HAVE A REMARKABLE TALENT FOR ACROBATICS.

Complementing the cat's sure sense of balance (see pages 42 to 44) are its flexible spine and strong muscles, along with the looseness of its skin and skeleton compared to ours. These features endow it with markedly more accomplished gymnastic skills than most humans can boast of. Some of the most notable differences between the feline and human skeleton are the forty extra bones that the feline's contains (mainly in the backbone and tail), along with the less rigid arrangement of the cat's vertebrae and the marked reduction in

clavicle (collarbone) size, which is compensated for by powerful muscles.

Combine a narrow physique, a head that can rotate more than 180 degrees, forelimbs whose length of stride can be greatly varied, a fluid backbone, highly muscled, springboard-like hindquarters and a tail whose position aids balance with an extraordinarily developed muscular system, all covered with loosely attached fur, and the result is both a formidable predator and a master of escapology.

FEW HUMANS WOULD DARE TO TREAD IN THE FOOTSTEPS OF A SURE-FOOTED FELINE.

As well as offering considerable advantages, the cat's body does, however, have its drawbacks, the inevitable consequence of the compromises that nature was forced to make when designing *Felis catus*. Because the wildcat was – and remains – an opportunistic predator that could not rely on a regular supply of food, for example, the stomach that its descendants have inherited takes up a disproportionately large amount of room at the expense of its heart and lungs. This means that although the cat has mastered the pouncing dash, its heart and lungs do not have the capacity to power any sustained form of exercise. It also explains why a well-fed house cat will frequently go off hunting virtually as soon as it has had its post-prandial wash and brush-up: it may not have digested its supper yet, but its ancestral programming tells it that it must be on the constant search for prey as an insurance against the lean times that could strike at any moment. Whether or not it actually eats its prey does, however, depend on how hungry it is.

Its physical inability to stalk its victims for long periods of time means that the cat has developed a less energy-consuming hunting strategy, that of lurking and waiting for prey, be it during the day or the night, according to

AFTER ITS EARS HAVE SIGNALLED THE PROXIMITY OF POS

BRINGS ITS EYESIGHT INTO PLAY.

when it has discovered that the locality's food supply is the most plentiful. Typically having taken up a covert position under a shrub – and preferably one that blends seamlessly with its coat to provide maximum camouflage – the cat will then patiently wait for a tasty morsel to cross its path.

As soon as it hears a tell-tale rustle or espies a sudden movement out of the corner of its eye, the cat's ears and eyes (see pages 45 to 48) spring into full-alert mode to monitor its quarry's progress as it prepares to pounce. Quivering with suppressed tension, the crouching cat fixes its eyes on its potential meal as it inches slowly towards it, sometimes freezing in mid-slink if it thinks that it may have been spotted. Once within pouncing distance, the cat springs forward for the kill, its hindquarters powering the leap while its front paws, razor-sharp claws unsheathed, reach out to pinion its prey to the ground before the deadly feline jaws close around the hapless victim's neck. If all goes smoothly, the cat's canine teeth (see pages 40 to 41) deliver the neck-breaking killing bite by dislocating its quarry's vertebrae, but if the execution proves problematic, it may rake the claws of its hindlegs along its prey's body, simultaneously

A SUDDEN MOVEMENT
CAUSES A CAT TO SNAP
INTO FULL-ALERT MODE.

KITTENS LEARN FROM THEIR MOTHERS

gripping and maiming as it seeks to administer the *coup de grâce* with its teeth.

Having won the life-or-death battle, before settling down to the feast, the cat will carry its quarry's corpse to a place that offers protective cover from other predators that may try to snatch its meal away from it. The reason why a cat will often proudly present its kills to its unappreciative owner is due to a number of factors, including how hungry it is. If it is ravenous, it will eat its prey, starting from the head. If its appetite is already sated, however, it may make a gift of its victim to its owner, probably because this is what a mother cat does when her kittens have been weaned. The house cat is thus providing both food and education for its human family: food, in that the fresh kill constitutes a 'proper' feline meal that it rarely – if ever – receives from its owners; and education, in that if its prey is still clinging on to life, the cat will often demonstrate to its owners how to dispatch it, just as a mother cat would instruct her kittens by example. (Although many people believe that when a cat 'toys' with a half-dead mouse it is being gratuitously cruel, this isn't so: it is simply practising its deadly skills in order to become a more proficient hunter.) So if you find yourself the recipient of such an unwanted gift and don't want to hurt your cat's feelings, first praise it profusely for its largesse and then discreetly dispose of your 'meal' when it isn't looking.

A tooth-and-claw fighter

As we have seen, in the final stages of the hunt the cat uses its claws to pin down its prey and its teeth to administer the killing bite. In non-aggressive mode, the cat's claws are retracted – or, more properly, sheathed – into the tips of its toe bones (the phalanges), both to prevent them from injuring itself or its friends and to preserve the sharpness of their points for, as every successful hunter or warrior knows, if you look

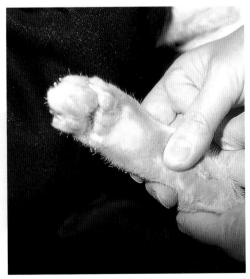

A CAT USUALLY KEEPS ITS CLAWS SHEATHED.

after your weapons, when it comes to the crunch they'll look after you. The cat's eighteen claws (four on each hind paw and five on each front paw, the fifth, called the dew claw, being higher up the paw) are made of a protein called keratin, the same substance that forms human nails. Like our nails, the feline's claws are constantly growing, the difference being that they are doing so beneath the existing set, so that when an elderly claw has outlived its usefulness, the cat will strop it off to reveal its fighting-fit replacement. (The process can loosely be compared to the way in which a

STROPPING KEEPS FELINE CLAWS FIGHTING FIT.

snake sloughs off its old skin.) Anchored firmly into the phalanges by rubbery ligaments, when the feline brain deems it prudent to unsheathe its primary weapons, further ligaments push the phalanges forward, and with them the claws, the process being performed at lightning speed, similar to the way in which a flick knife is activated. Once in contact with its prey, the claws relay positional information regarding how effectively the cat is twisting them, as well as the suitability of the pressure that it is using, enabling it to readjust its clawhold if necessary.

If the cat's claws can be roughly equated with human nails, the padded cushions of hairless skin at the bottom of its paws can be described as being equivalent to the palms of our hands and the soles of our feet. The softness of the paw pads in comparison to, for example, the hooves of non-predatory creatures like the horse, muffles the cat's approach, giving it the advantage of surprise when stalking. Only when its paws have carried the cat close enough to pounce are the claws unsheathed in readiness for their deadly mission.

Perhaps rather insultingly to the feline community's pride, the teeth that close in for the kill are termed the canines, the fangs that can be seen on either side of the cat's miniature incisors. Being sensitive to pressure, as well as extremely sharp, they enable the cat to judge exactly where to sink them in order to dislocate its victim's vertebrae and cause its instantaneous death. Once it has dispatched its quarry using this swift and effective method, the same teeth are used to tear at the corpse to expose the warm flesh beneath the fur or feathers, the more delicate scraping and ripping work being done by the incisors. The molars, and particularly the sideways-slicing carnassials, at the back of the cat's mouth now come into

their own by reducing the flesh to bite-sized chunks. Unlike our flattened molars, the cat's back teeth have sharp tips that speed up the food-preparation process (another legacy of its wildcat heritage, in that felines are programmed to eat as quickly as possible in case their meal is snatched away by another predator that has been attracted by the smell of the kill). And, again in contrast to human eating patterns, the cat does not pre-digest its food by chewing it thoroughly before swallowing, instead leaving most of the digestive process to its stomach's gastric juices.

THE THRILL OF THE CHASE – CATS CAN ATTAIN A TOP SPEED OF AROUND 30 MILES (48 KM) AN HOUR.

41

An acrobat's skills

A cat climbs like a monkey, walks as gracefully as a ballerina and balances with the effortless ease of a champion tightrope-walker. As we have seen, when a cat is hunting, its powerful back legs provide the momentum that launches it into a leap or pounce, while its front legs stretch out to grasp its prey. This pattern is repeated when a cat climbs a vertical object like a tree or fence, its hindquarters propelling it upwards – sometimes up to five times the cat's height – and the hooked claws of its front paws sinking into the surface to act as grappling irons, thereby enabling the cat to get a firm enough hold to pull itself upwards with its strong front legs.

The delicate elegance of the cat's walk is the result of the configuration of its leg and paw bones, which differs from the way in which human legs and feet are constructed. Your leg consists of a thighbone (femur), knee and, beneath that, a parallel shinbone (tibia) and fibula, then comes the ankle joint above the heelbone (calcaneus), in front of which is the large talus bone, followed by a series of smaller bones that culminate in the metatarsals and finally the phalanges, the toe bones. In contrast to us, the cat walks on the tips of its phalanges, which are far longer than human toe bones, while its leg bones are shorter. Not only does this 'digitigrade' arrangement allow a longer stride, it enables the cat to run far faster than if its feet were 'plantigrade' like ours. Balancing on the tips of its toes, the cat walks in a diagonal fashion by putting forward its left hindleg first, followed by its right foreleg, its right hindleg and finally its left foreleg, before stepping out with its left hindleg again, positioning each front or back paw directly in front of the previous one on the same side so that if you examined its tracks in the snow (that is, if you could persuade it to consent to having its feet frozen in the first place), they would form two straight lines. Again, it is the cat's powerful hindquarters that provide the ambulatory momentum, while its front legs support the weight of its head. This way of walking can be varied to enable the cat to break out into a trot or gallop, and it has been estimated that the cat can attain a top speed of around 30 miles (48 km) an hour.

HAVING DECIDED THAT IT'S TIME TO MOVE FROM ITS COMFORTABLE POSITION, THE SEATED CAT BEGINS THE DESCENT, ITS FRONT LEGS LEADING THE WAY, WITH ITS HINDQUARTERS PROVIDING THE AMBULATORY MOMENTUM.

The precise, economical feline gait is of considerable help when it comes to performing an intricate balancing act along a wall or fence, as is the tail in correcting potential imbalances, but that's only part of the story. Having scrambled onto the wall, once it is again moving horizontally, the cat's brain is guided by its vestibular organ, which relays positional information that enables the cat to adjust its movements if necessary to forestall a tumble. Although the cat's vestibular organ is situated in the inner ear, as in the human body, its performance is remarkably superior to its human counterpart, and not only as regards balance: unlike many people, cats never suffer from motion sickness, for instance. The vestibular organ comprises three hair-lined, fluid-filled, semi-circular canals that are arranged at right angles to each other. When the cat moves its head, the fluid in one canal responds to up-and-down motions, another to left-and-right movements and the third to oblique positions, the movement of the fluid being detected by the adjacent hairs and reported to the brain. The crystalline saccular and utricular otolith organs represent further refinements of the vestibular organ that register gravity on the one hand and speed of movement on the other. Each of the vestibular system's components works instantaneously, together sending an array of reflexive signals to the feline brain, as well as to the muscles that are instrumental in maintaining balance, that report the position of the cat's head in relation to the ground and therefore enable it to correct any false move. If the cat does fall, however, the workings of this system allow it to recover in mid-air, to correct the position of its head and to prepare itself for a safe landing by twisting its body so that its shock-absorbing legs will be the first to hit the ground, also arching its back to minimise the shock of the impact and stretching out its tail to act as a counterbalance. The cat's ability to right itself is amazing in itself, but what is perhaps even more astonishing is that this complex set of manouevres is performed in less than the blink of an eye.

CATS BOAST SUPER-DEVELOPED BALANCING SKILLS.

The feline senses

Apart from its sense of taste (and as a carnivore it has no need for the luxury of a gourmet's appreciation of the delicacies of flavour – fresh meat is, after all, fresh meat, although shrews must taste really disgusting because it appears that only the most ravenous cat will consume them), the functioning and powers of the feline's senses are generally far superior to ours. They need to be, for in its natural state the cat relies on them for its very life.

Citing the saying that cats have nine lives (and, indeed, many stroll away from hair-raising scrapes virtually unscathed), some people believe that the cat is guided through life by a sixth sense, also known as extra-sensory perception. Although there is, as yet, no compelling scientific evidence to confirm this, it is thought that cats, in common with many animals, are far more sensitive both to electrical changes in the atmosphere and the earth's magnetic field. This may explain on the one hand why many cats become uneasy at the approach of an electrical storm or earthquake and, on the other, why some cats who have been forcibly relocated, perhaps because their human family has moved house, have an uncanny ability to find their way back to their old home. Generally, however, their conventional sensory perceptions are more than adequate to enable them to survive and thrive.

Hearing and the cat's ears

MOBILE FELINE EARS RESEMBLE RADAR DETECTORS.

Its hearing is the first sense that alerts the cat to potential prey when it is out hunting and, due to its genetic inheritance, the sounds that are most likely to signal the proximity of rodents, its favourite meal, are the ones to which it is the most attuned. And because rodents utter high-pitched squeaks, the upper frequencies of the sound range are those that the cat's ears are especially adept at detecting, exceeding both

dogs and humans in their sensitivity. Indeed, when you think that our detection of acoustic vibrations rises to around 20,000 hertz, and a cat's to 50,000, we must be deaf to a cacophony of interesting sounds.

Watch any cat, whether it is lurking with murderous intent or deeply relaxed, and you will often see its ears suddenly spring into action, whether or not you can hear the noise that prompted them to go into a state of full alert. Initially you may see its funnel-shaped ear 'lobes' (pinnae), which, with their sweeping range of 180 degrees are remarkably mobile, as well as designed to amplify sound, swivelling (often independently of each other) in much the same way as a radar detector as they attempt to pinpoint the precise location of the trigger sound. This process is accomplished within the middle and inner ears, which vibrate in reaction to the frequency of the sound that has been picked up, causing the nerve cells within the ears to relay the information detected to the cat's brain. Having received differing messages from each ear, their subsequent comparison enables the feline brain to calculate the positional source of the tantalising noise. Corresponding to the frequencies of sound emitted by rodents, this direction-finding method

is usually more successful with higher registers than with lower ones (and explains why cats are typically more responsive to women's voices than to men's), when the cat will be forced to bring its eyesight into play.

Seeing and the cat's eyes

BINOCULAR VISION AIDS A CAT'S FOCUSING POWER.

Once the exact location of an interesting sound has been identified by its ears, the cat directs its eyes in that direction to try to identify its source. This may take a little time if the culprit rodent, for example, has spotted the cat and has frozen, or else is moving slowly, because feline eyes are genetically programmed to respond primarily to sudden movements and to focus on objects that are moving either quickly or erratically, as would its prey when trying to outmanoeuvre and escape it. (To observe the cause and effect of this instinct, all you need to do is watch a cat trying to catch a butterfly.) Indeed, the cat's eyes are in every respect those of a predator, being both extremely large in comparison to the size of its skull, in order maximise its visual capabilities, and set at the front of the head, facing forwards. In contrast to the eyes of creatures that are typically preyed upon, such as rabbits, which are positioned on either side of the head, giving them sideways monocular (one-eyed) vision in each direction, the better to scan a wide area for potential predators, the cat's binocular (two-eyed) vision is designed to enable it to focus intently on a tasty-looking victim, the image registered by each eye overlapping with the other to give a detailed, stereoscopic view that results in a three-dimensional image. While the size and generous curve of the cat's eyes give them a visual scope of up to 285 degrees, their range is further extended by the impressive swivelling capability of the neck, which means that the cat's eyes can cover a wide area without its body having to move to any great extent – an invaluable asset when operating under cover.

SAUCER EYES EQUAL SUPERIOR SIGHT.

No cover is more effective than that of darkness and, its African ancestors having bequeathed *Felis catus* the gift of night vision, most cats will go out to hunt at night if they can. Although they can't actually discern objects in total darkness (for, as every photographer knows, an image cannot be recorded in the total absence of light), and it takes some time for their eyes to adjust to the dark, they can still see at least six times better than humans in dusky conditions. This is due to three factors: firstly, their ability to vary the size of their pupils to a considerable degree; secondly, the teeming population of rods (three times greater in number than in the

human eye) that the feline eye contains; and, thirdly, the tapetum lucidum that is located at the back of the eye. In response to the dark of night, the cat's pupils widen enormously to form a full circle (during the day they can be narrowed from slits to pinpricks to protect the eye from dangerous dazzle, the nictitating membrane, also known as the haw, or 'third eyelid', being enlisted in extreme conditions), which maximises the amount of available light that enters the eye. Once the light has passed into the eye, it is focused by the lens to form an image on the retina, which is picked up by receptor cells called rods (whose job is to 'switch on' the cat's night vision by registering the intensity of light), which then transmit it to the brain via the optic nerve. Some light may have eluded the rods, however, in which case it continues to travel forward, beyond the retina to the tapetum lucidum (the Latin for 'bright mirror'), fifteen layers of flat, reflective cells that deflect the light the way it came, giving the rods another chance to register it and send it on to the brain. (It is light bouncing off the tapetum lucidum that gives the luminous shine to the eyes of creatures of the night that in 1934 inspired Percy Shaw to invent the cat's-eyes that today guide drivers along the roads at night by reflecting the light emitted by their headlights.)

There are a few disadvantages inherent in the feline night-stalker's vision, however. One is that the cat's eyes contain fewer cones (the receptor cells responsible for sending messages to the brain to enable the eyes to focus in daylight) than ours, which means that it does not see as clearly as we do during the day. And because it is also cones that are responsible for distinguishing colours, although cats are not colour blind, it is thought that they do not discern different shades and hues as well as we do. However, neither ability is particularly important when *Felis catus* is out hunting at night. Another drawback is the difficulty that cats have in focusing on objects that are less than 15 centimetres (6 inches) away. Caspar, for example, who is partial to the occasional peanut, cannot see where one has fallen when it is tossed in front of his nose onto our similarly coloured floor because he cannot distinguish between nuances of shade and there is insufficient contrast for him to be able to identify the peanut's shape. This is not, however, a major handicap, for Caspar, like every cat, is able to call on his senses of touch and smell to lead him directly to the peanut.

Touching and the cat's tactile receptors

WHEN FACED WITH AN UNFAMILIAR OBJECT, A CAT WILL USUALLY FIRST INVESTIGATE IT WITH A TENTATIVE PAW.

Whether it be an immobile peanut, a living victim or any other object that the cat considers worthy of more detailed exploration, the feline has an armoury of sensitive touch receptors at its clawtips – and not only there. You may have seen a curious cat tentatively patting an object – perhaps a new toy mouse – with its paw. Although it may look comical, the cat isn't playing, but is instead conducting a serious investigation. After all, it doesn't yet know that this alien object is a toy – it doesn't show signs of life, but that doesn't mean that it won't jump up and bite the cat on the nose. With caution being the watchword, the cat therefore extends a forepaw, keeping its vulnerable nose well away from the potential danger, and delicately touches the toy mouse. The instant it does so, a barrage of messages is relayed to the brain by the touch receptors – nerve endings – in the hairless pads of its paw, which are activated by

sideways, brushing movements similar to those that the cat is generating as it pats and strokes. (So sensitive are the paw pads that many cats hate having them stroked – Melchior certainly does, although Caspar tolerates it – presumably because it elicits a tickling sensation that is too excruciating to stand.) Only when the feline brain has ascertained that the toy mouse doesn't present a threat will the cat draw closer to investigate it with its nose, which is equally chock-a-block with touch receptors, both

touching and smelling the mouse to garner as much information as it can. If the toy were a real mouse, this closeness of contact would trigger an innate set of killer reactions in which further touch receptors under the skin of the mouth and lips play a vital role in prompting the cat to bare its fangs ready for the killing bite, the final information that seals the mouse's fate being relayed by nerve endings within the mouth and pressure-sensitive receptors at the base of the canine teeth.

NOT EVEN A COMPUTER MOUSE CAN ESCAPE THIS CAT'S CURIOSITY.

RECEPTORS AT THE BASE OF THE CANINE TEETH RELAY DATA TO THE FELINE PREDATOR'S BRAIN.

Beneath its fur the feline skin is packed with touch receptors (which is one of the reasons why cats are so responsive to being stroked), but certain areas are more sensitive than others – around the cat's mouth, for example. Among the most responsive to touch are the vibrissae: the whiskers and stiff, whisker-like hairs that sprout from above a cat's eyes, from its chin and the sides of its head, as well as from the 'wrists' of its paws. Not only do the vibrissae register touch when they come into contact with a solid object, thereby acting as feelers, they also identify changes in air pressure, even the most imperceptible (to humans) movement

CATS ADORE BEING STROKED.

looking gap.

Never cut off a cat's whiskers, for if you do, you will be inflicting a considerable handicap on it by removing its ability to make accurate spatial judgments and will also probably be condemning any future prey to a lingering death as a result of the cat's impaired ability to judge exactly where to administer the *coup de grâce*.

causing the vibrissae to bend and triggering a brain-signalling response in the touch receptors at their base, within the skin. Because solid objects affect the air flow or pressure around them, the cat is alerted to their presence and can therefore avoid them. As well as enabling it to map out the size and shape of any object that the cat encounters (including the prey that it holds in a death grip), the vibrissae provide an invaluable navigational aid, giving the cat the ability to ascertain with remarkable accuracy, particularly during its night-time sorties, whether it can squeeze through a prohibitively small-

THE CAT'S WHISKERS TRIGGER TOUCH RECEPTORS.

Tasting and the cat's tongue

The feline senses are generally far more sensitive than those of humans, but there is one that compares relatively badly to ours: the cat's sense of taste. Although some cats are said to be fussy eaters, this has less to do with their ability to distinguish subtle nuances of flavour and is more concerned with the freshness of the food offered to them: they distrust the smell of stale, or even rotting, food, having the instinctive knowledge that it could make them ill. Another reason for the refusal on the part of *Felis catus* – a creature of habit – to countenance any food to which it is not accustomed is the legacy of its usually unvarying carnivorous diet in the wild. Indeed, many owners find that a cat that turns its nose up at a certain type of proprietary canned cat food will not be able to resist a morsel of fresh flesh of any type, be it meat, fish or poultry.

Its innate preference for fresh meat aside, there are also certain biological explanations for the cat's likes and dislikes when it comes to food. The human palate, which boasts eighteen times more taste buds than the feline's, is not only far more sensitive to different tastes, but more tolerant of the four cardinal flavours: sour, bitter, salt and sweet. This is because humans are omnivores and have therefore become

FEW CATS CAN RESIST A MEAT-BASED MEAL, AS LONG AS IT IS FRESH AND DOESN'T SMELL STALE.

accustomed over the course of many millennia to eating plants and other food stuffs, as well as meat. The carnivorous cat, by contrast, will shrink from the acidity of a sour citrus fruit and will wrinkle its nose at the bitterness of a particular herb – and neither flavour occurs naturally in meat – in addition appearing indifferent to salt, presumably because meat contains all of this nutrient that its body needs, and hardly seeming to register sweetness because sugar does not form part of a feline's nutritional requirements.

Indeed, the only flavours that are pertinent to a feline's nutritional needs are those of meat and fat, which supply it with tissue-maintaining protein and storable energy, and these are the ones that are registered by the cat's taste buds, which are mainly located on the edges of the tongue. The centre of the tongue contains the papillae (tiny, backward-pointing hooks) that trap the water that the cat drinks when it is moderately thirsty or when only a thin layer of water is available. When a feline has a powerful thirst, however, or the water source is deep, it will form its tongue into a shape resembling a spoon, thus enabling it to ladle larger quantities of water down its throat.

THE ONLY TASTES THAT A CAT TRULY APPRECIATES ARE THOSE OF MEAT AND FAT.

Smelling and the cat's nose

Although how its food smells determines whether or not a cat will eat it, the feline nose is a far more versatile organ of smell than simply a food-identifier. Indeed, it plays a crucial role in feline relationships – both sexual and social – and if a cat's sense of smell is impaired for any reason, it may start to behave in a most unfeline way.

Because their noses contain twice as large an area containing smell receptors (hosting around 19 million nerve endings) than humans (our noses contain about 5 million), cats are significantly more sensitive to smell than we are. The reason why many cats, to their owners' despair, prefer drinking from unhygienic-looking puddles to the water bowl that has been provided for them, for example, is because they are repelled by the smell of the chemicals with which many water companies treat tap water (although they are barely detectable to us, if at all), and may also dislike the lingering odour of the washing-up liquid – another unnatural-smelling substance – that may have been used to clean the bowl.

THE FELINE NOSE IS CHOCK-A-BLOCK WITH BOTH TOUCH RECEPTORS AND SMELL RECEPTORS.

A CAT SWAPS SCENT SIGNALS WITH ITS OWNER.

to the Jacobson's organ, which consists of two sacs, opened by the cat's flehming, that contain receptors that pick up the odour and report it to the cat's brain for analysis.

When a cat rubs its head or chin against your leg or hand, it is not simply demonstrating how much it loves you, but is both marking you as its property and exchanging scent signals with you. Along with those situated on the feline's temples, chin and at the corners of its lips, there are sebaceous glands at the base of its tail and around its anus that produce the cat's own,

And it is not just to the odours emitted by food and water that cats react strongly, the scent of a female cat on heat, for instance, attracting toms from quite some distance away, with the toms increasing their spraying rate in response. It is thought to be primarily sexual scent signals that are responsible for the peculiar face that cats of both sexes occasionally pull, whereby they raise their upper lip and open their mouths to expose their incisors, their eyes all the while displaying a distant, dreamy expression. Known as 'flehming', this unmistakable grimace enables a particularly tantalising scent to pass through a duct in the roof of the mouth behind the incisors

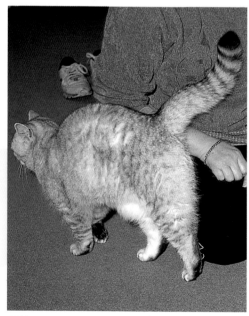

SEBACEOUS GLANDS EMIT A CAT'S UNIQUE SCENT.

unique smell. In rubbing against you, it is transferring its individual scent to your skin or clothing, and when it pulls away and embarks on a vigorous washing session, it is not insulting you by trying to remove all traces of your body odour from its fur as fast as it can – although it may certainly be trying to restore its own

A CARPET MAY HAVE A FASCINATING STORY TO TELL.

THE FELINE NOSE IS AN INSTRUMENT OF DETECTION.

fragrant status quo – but is enabling the taste buds on its tongue to savour your personal taste. Such exchanges of scent are crucial in reinforcing the shared 'family' smell that makes a cat feel at home. Similarly, when a cat insists on sniffing your hand or clothes with rapt fascination, it is 'reading' scent messages that tell it where you have been, what you have been doing, and with whom. Sadly, we are largely oblivious to the richness of the cat's vocabulary of scent and, indeed, find it difficult to imagine the extent to which a feline's life is both regulated and enhanced by smell.

The cat's social life

THIS CAT IS IN THE PROCESS OF SCENT-MARKING ITS TERRITORY.

As well as controlling the essential functions of eating, drinking and breeding, in many respects the feline sense of smell can be said to be the engine that keeps cat society running smoothly, defining as it does the individual cat's place within its feline (or feline–human) community, its relationship with other cats (or, in the case of a human household, surrogate cats) and the boundaries of its personal territory.

Despite the prevalent belief that cats prefer a solitary existence (and they certainly don't hunt in packs as wolves do, for example), observers of feral felines – cats that have reverted to a wild lifestyle – have noted that they tend to live in groups, mainly consisting of females and their offspring. Such cat communes operate along communist lines, with the females often sharing out the job of nurturing and raising kittens. Toms, however, are usually conspicuous by their absence, partly because they are polygamous by habit and rarely stay with one family group for long before moving on to bestow their favours upon another, and partly because much of their time is spent securing and defending their territory from other male marauders. Every cat has its place within the feline community, largely determined by the powerfulness of the scent of its sex hormones: the tom, who has fought and vanquished another tom to establish his status, is the top cat; queens, or actively breeding females, rank next, followed by other females; while the kittens' place is at the bottom of the heap. A good part of a cat's kittenhood is spent scrapping with its littermates in an attempt to gain precedence, and when young males have become sexually mature they will either challenge the dominant tom for control of the group or leave the community in search of their own territory. Neutering, which results in a decrease in sex hormones and therefore their odour, heralds a dramatic loss of status for cats, neutered cats being immediately relegated to the bottom of the social ladder.

THE BATTLE FOR PRECEDENCE IS AN IMPORTANT PART OF KITTENHOOD.

A KITTEN PRACTISES LEAPING AND POUNCING.

The cat's two most vital requirements are food and shelter, and once it has found a place, or household, that offers both it will come to regard both it and its immediate environs, such as a garden, as its personal territory that it must defend against interlopers at all costs. Because this strict territorial division isn't always practical or possible in densely populated localities, there may some areas, such as streets, that the neighbourhood's cats deem neutral zones (although they usually avoid coming into

contact with other felines there), while others will be designated feline meeting places, rather like human cafés. Generally, however, every cat regards its core living space as its kingdom and will not tolerate it being threatened by any cat that is not part of its immediate feline or human family. Just as we enclose our gardens with gates and fences, the cat does much the same around its home turf, although its 'Keep out!'

THE GREAT OUTDOORS IS TEEMING WITH THE FELINE SCE

notices are the intangible ones of scent, which you will often see a tom depositing by spraying his urine, tail aquiver as he directs it backwards, on certain points around his realm's boundaries. (And if even we, with our inferior sense of smell, recoil from the pungent odour of a tom's urine, imagine what effect it has on a fellow feline.) All cats mark their territory with their smell, be it via their urine or their scent glands (by rubbing their heads against trees, for example), refreshing their personal fragrance regularly as it fades. You will often see a cat pausing and reflectively sniffing a plant or garden feature as it 'reads' another feline's message, occasionally adding a fragrant footnote of its own so that a subsequent visitor will know that it has been there.

Although a cat will unhesitatingly defend its territory against feline intruders (and it prefers to do this by means of deterrence rather than direct confrontation), its relationship with those that it lives with – its family, be they blood relations or not, fellow cats or humans – is far less aggressive. Having left behind kittenhood, when playing games with other kittens served both as an education in hunting skills and established each kitten's place in the feline pecking order, cats become increasing aloof from one another as they mature. Certain feline interactions remain important, however, in maintaining the bond between cats that live together. One is mutual rubbing and grooming sessions, in which scents are exchanged and feelings of trust are reinforced. And when one cat returns to its home base from a border patrol, its curious housemates will often sniff its head and tail avidly to ascertain from its scent

◄ MARK THE BOUNDARIES OF A CAT'S KINGDOM.

A DOMINANT CAT INITIATES A SCRAP, PROMPTING ITS HOUSEMATE TO BEAT A HASTY RETREAT.

what it has been up to while it was away. Usually it is an inferior cat who initiates rubbing, sniffing and grooming sessions, probably as a way of ensuring that it retains the superior cat's friendship, or at least tolerance, and this may also explain why cats prefer to approach their owners (whom they regard as boss cats) for some affectionate interaction rather than the other way round, which breaches feline etiquette.

The cat's powers of communication

As well as transmitting and receiving scent messages, cats communicate volumes by means of their body language and vocalisation.

MAKING ITSELF LOOK SMALLER SIGNIFIES SUBMISSION.

The feline body – particularly the ears and tail – is a highly expressive instrument that instantly communicates how a cat is feeling within its skin if only you know how to interpret the keynotes. The emotional signal that is perhaps the easiest for humans to recognise is fear. When threatened by a more dominant cat with hostile intent which it has no desire to fight, the undercat will nevertheless stand its ground, albeit flattening its body, fur and ears in an attempt to make itself look as small and inoffensive as it can, shortly thereafter beginning to creep slowly backwards as it tries to remove itself from danger. All the while, the more aggressive cat, its pupils contracted into slits, will be trying to stare down the other feline with unblinking concentration – an aggressive action in cat language – while the other cat, pupils dilated and blinking in response, will be trying to convey the message, through its avoidance of eye contact, that it means no harm. These gestures signal submission, and if all goes well and the aggressor decides not to pursue the undercat, it will be able to slink away, all the while keeping a wary eye on its tormentor. If, on the other hand, the felines are evenly matched, a staring match may take place that may last for a considerable time, with, to the human eye, very little happening apart from some hisses and growls. A battle of wills is, in fact, taking place, which, if neither feline gives in, may well escalate and end either with them swiping at each other with their forepaws or in a claw-flashing, fur-flying fight, during which the losing cat may be forced to roll onto its back, both to protect its neck from the killing bite and to enable it to lash out with its powerful hindlegs. The end of the scrap is signalled with the loser lying flat on the ground and the victor apparently losing interest, perhaps turning away and sniffing raptly at a nearby spot, a contemptuous gesture intended to convey the message that its vanquished opponent no longer poses any sort of threat.

A CAT'S BODY LANGUAGE BETRAYS ITS INTENTION TO POUNCE.

the feline world

Cats usually prefer to resolve their differences by means of psychological warfare than risk being injured, and you will probably have seen many variations on the aggressive–submissive body-language theme. Another defensive message, for instance, is signalled by what is known as the 'arched-back' posture beloved of cartoonists, which is typically enacted in response to the danger of an imminent attack by a truly dangerous foe – a dog, for example. The cat's primary intention in assuming this position is to make itself look larger and more formidable, thereby trying to trick the dog into believing that it would be no pushover in a fight. It accordingly arches its back by stiffening its limbs, pointing its forelegs backwards and its hindlegs forwards, and raising its tail to increase its height, also fluffing up the fur on its body and tail (which it may sometimes curve into a hooped shape) to make itself appear wider and more substantial. If the situation is looking really desperate, it may furthermore resort to the diversionary tactic of hissing, growling and making explosive spitting sounds in an attempt

FELINE CONFRONTATION TACTICS INCLUDE MANY VARIATIONS ON THE AGGRESSIVE–SUBMISSIVE THEME.

to startle the dog and thus break its concentration, giving the cat a breathing space in which to escape. (Most animals are at the very least wary of snakes, if not terrified of them, and it is probably no coincidence that a cornered cat's hiss, followed by spitting, resembles the warning sounds made by a serpent. This association may also explain why many cats flee when an aerosol can is squirted and why Melchior makes himself scarce when the steam iron's switched on.)

Actual feline fisticuffs aside, signs of aggression or confidence are less easy for human observers to spot, that is, unless they are versed in the vocabulary of the feline body language.

If a cat is in the mood to initiate a showdown, it signals its intent by stalking stiffly towards its chosen opponent. Once it has come within staring distance, it will concentrate every part of its body on its victim. The tip of its tail may twitch, betraying the tension that it is experiencing, but its ears will be pricked, albeit protectively pulled back, as it stares intently at its rival. With luck, that will be enough to cow the other cat into submission, and off the boss cat will then strut, with its tail held high, looking inordinately pleased with itself.

CONFIDENCE IS SIGNALLED BY ERECT EARS AND A STEADY GAZE.

Indeed, you can tell a lot by looking at a cat's tail and ears: if its tail is vertical and its ears are pricked, the cat is feeling confident, and if the tip of its erect tail is kinked, it's offering you a tentative greeting. When a cat turns its back on you and quivers its tail, it's sending an unreserved, 'Please acknowledge me' plea that may well hark back to a kittenhood invitation to its mother to clean its nether regions. If a cat is becoming annoyed, however, it often indicates its frustration by swishing its tail from side to side and drawing back its ears, and if it becomes really irate, it will lash its tail as fast as it can and flatten its ears completely.

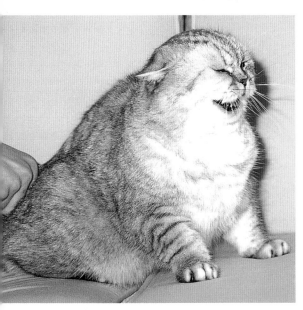

FLATTENED EARS DENOTE A REALLY RATTLED CAT.

The final chapter in the beginner's guide to feline communication consists of the various sounds that a cat makes. As we have seen, cats that find themselves in situations of potential conflict often resort to issuing warning growls, hisses and explosive spits, signals that are often interspersed with low wails and harsh snarls. If the conflict escalates, a torrent of ear-splitting yowls and caterwauls may be unleashed, as well as the occasional shriek of pain if a sharp claw sinks into soft flesh. Such unfriendly noises signify both aggression and deterrence, the intention being to make the foe think that the cat will prove such a formidable opponent that it would be wiser not to attempt an attack. At night especially, loud, unearthly wails may rend the air – these are the call-and-response yowls initiated by the vocal invitations of females on heat and the toms' answering 'mowls', although because all of the neighbourhood's toms are likely to have hot-footed it in the female's direction, some will be the aggressive noises made by a tom facing down a rival.

The conversational sounds that a cat makes are far quieter, as well as more musical, than those that it produces in response to the crises of warfare or sex. A queen communicates with her kittens using a variety of coos, trills and

A MOTHER CAT USES A RANGE OF GENTLE SOUNDS TO COMMUNICATE WITH HER BROOD.

chirrups, all of which quickly become part of a kitten's vocal repertoire that it retains when it grows into adulthood. Be it to greet, encourage, chivvy, make a request or simply to express how a cat is feeling, these gentle sounds have many purposes, and each cat's use of them is unique. To the human ear, the cat's most familiar sound is, of course, the miaow, or mew, a feline word that has entered the vocabulary of many human languages: *mau* in Egyptian, *naoua* in Arabic, *myaus* in India, *mio* in China, *miaou* in France and *Miau* in Germany, to give just a few examples. Interestingly, most cats miaow more at humans than at fellow felines, which has led some researchers to believe that the miaow and its various nuances may be the cat's attempt to imitate human speech and therefore to initiate a conversation that humans are more likely to understand than the feline language, in which humans are, of course, near-illiterates.

BY MIAOWING, IS A CAT TRYING TO SPEAK 'HUMAN'?

control. (Caspar, for example, often does this when he's being examined by the vet, who is not his favourite person, despite the vet's gentle hands and demeanour, when it could also be a interpreted as plea for kindly treatment.)

The feline sounds discussed above are all made consciously, unlike purring, which is an involuntary response. Typically made when a cat is feeling relaxed and contented – while being stroked, for instance – the low, rumbling sound that is characteristic of the purr is generally thought to be produced as the air that the cat breathes in and out passes over a pair of vestibular folds (false vocal cords) in the throat, the sound thereby generated being amplified by the vibration of the larynx as its muscles relax and contract. Despite its general association with contentment, a cat may also purr frantically when it finds itself in an uncomfortable plight, a paradoxical response that may be a feline attempt either to reassure or distract itself from fear of being a situation over which it has no

A CONTENTED CAT PURRS AUTOMATICALLY.

ITS REGULAR BOUNDARY PATROLS HELP TO KEEP AN OUTDOOR CAT FIT AND TRIM.

Feline self-maintenance

A successful hunter needs to be fit, and cats keep themselves trim by strolling the perimeters of their territory on their regular inspection tours, climbing trees or other lofty vantage points from which they can monitor any interesting goings-on and, of course, pouncing at potential prey. (The reason why many indoor cats occasionally career around the house at top speed is both to let off steam and to indulge in the type of hunting exercise that outdoor cats more regularly enjoy.)

Exploratory or deadly mission having been accomplished, it's then time for the cat to give itself a thorough wash and brush-up before

A LOFTY VANTAGE POINT GIVES AN INQUISITIVE CAT A BIRD'S-EYE VIEW OF ITS SURROUNDINGS.

settling down to enjoy a well-earned snooze. All animals, humans included, need to keep themselves clean if they are to remain healthy, and cats are particularly scrupulous when it comes to personal hygiene. Unlike humans, cats don't have sweat glands (apart from some in their paw pads), which means that it is difficult for them to keep cool in hot weather. (Although they generally like to bask in a sunny spot, their preferred response to soaring temperatures is to find the coolest available spot to lie in and then to stay prone, declining to participate in any heat-generating, energetic pursuits. If heatstroke threatens, they will either lick their fur, the saliva cooling their bodies as it evaporates, or, in extreme cases, pant.) The absence of sweat glands, however, means that their personal ablutions are less concerned with cleansing than with grooming; excising their body odour – their personal hallmark – is anathema to felines. Cats also wash as a displacement activity. If a cat finds itself in an agony of confusion, or feels that it has suffered a loss of dignity, it will often lick its flanks vigorously, partly to give itself time to recover its self-composure and partly to save face and make it appear purposeful instead of baffled.

HEAD DEALT WITH, THE FORELIMBS ARE NEXT UP . . .

. . . FOLLOWED BY THE FLANKS . . .

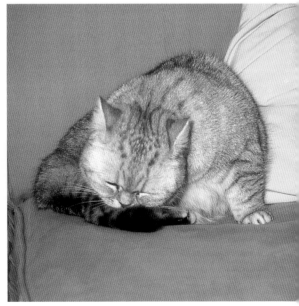

. . . AND, FINALLY, THE TAIL.

What the feline tongue lacks in the way of taste buds, it more than makes up for with its plethora of hooked papillae (see page 54) that serve as an essential grooming aid. Although you may think that a cat is washing in the human sense when you see it licking its fur, it is actually combing its coat, which, depending on its breed, generally consists of three layers: the short, soft down hairs nearest the skin, then the slightly longer and thicker awn hairs (both types insulating the feline body against the cold) and finally the even longer and coarser guard hairs that make up the protective topcoat. Working from the head to the tail, as the barbed papillae move over the surface of the coat, they remove any superficial tangles, as well as hairs that are

A CAT MOISTENS A FOREPAW AS IT PREPARES TO WASH ITS FACE.

no longer firmly embedded within the skin – dead hairs – thereby encouraging new growth. More stubborn clumps of tangled fur are nibbled out with the incisor teeth, which a cat also uses to pull off its old 'toenails' which, unlike its front claws, it cannot strop away against a tree. Despite the impressive revolving capability of the feline neck, which allows it to take care of its back, it can't give a feline tongue access to its nape or head, and cats therefore give these areas a good scrub by rubbing them with a pre-licked forepaw, following a precise routine. And when it comes to gaining access to the feline nether regions, cats demonstrate an innate talent for yoga with their ability to raise an obstructive hindleg to the vertical position.

CATS TAKE CLEANLINESS VERY SERIOUSLY.

Because cats spend so much time washing and bury their faeces, too, many people approvingly regard them as being fastidiously clean creatures. Although this is undeniably so, there are more reasons underlying the feline's fetish for hygiene than simply the desire to keep itself, as well as its surroundings, spick and span. Covering over faeces with earth does, of course, prevent the spread of disease, but perhaps a more important benefit to the feline is that this procedure reduces the likelihood of the faeces' smell either guiding an enemy to its whereabouts, especially the home in which it feels safe, or alerting potential prey to its presence and sending them scuttling away. Studies have provided support for this theory, it

IT IS NOT ONLY FOR REASONS OF HYGIENE THAT CATS, UNLIKE DOGS, BURY THEIR FAECES.

having been observed that immature and neutered cats, who are at the bottom of the feline social stratum, are more rigorous faeces-buriers than toms and queens, who have a better chance of successfully defending themselves against hostile interlopers and of catching elusive quarry.

As for any animal, sleep is vital for the cat, this down-time enabling it to recharge its batteries and giving its body the necessary peace and quiet in which to digest food and carry out tissue maintenance without the distraction of external stimuli. And the reason why cats sleep so much – typically for around 16 hours out of every 24 – is to conserve energy in preparation

for their intense, night-time forays. Like ours, the cat's sleep is divided into two distinct phases: light and deep. You can tell when a cat is sleeping lightly – having a catnap – because it will have curled up in a comfortable spot, with its tail curved around its body and its head tucked in neatly. Despite appearances, it is still in a state of alertness, ready to respond to any interesting sound (try giving a high whistle and see its ears prick up in response) and to spring into action if necessary.

A disconcerting sight to the human observer, sometimes a cat will sleep with its eyes open, with its third eyelids pulled across the surface of its eyes to seal in moisture. When its body is lying at full stretch and has become completely floppy, the cat has entered a deep sleep. And if you see a paw, ear or whisker twitch, your feline friend is in all likelihood enjoying an action-packed dream in which it is reliving hunting triumphs, analysis of the brainwaves of sleeping cats having shown marked similarities to those of humans during the dream state.

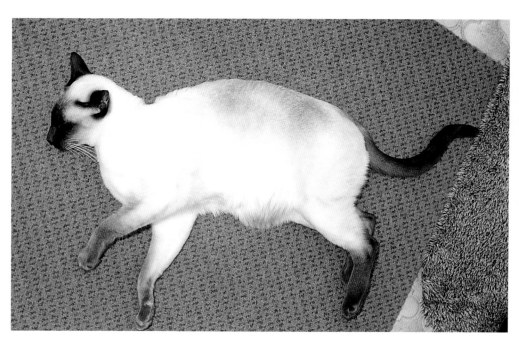

SLEEP IS SO IMPORTANT FOR A FELINE THAT MOST CATS SPEND TWO-THIRDS OF THE DAY SNOOZING.

2

Adopting a cat

adopting a cat

Making the decision to adopt a cat – or cats – should not be taken lightly, so think long and hard before impulsively taking home an irresistibly appealing kitten who has melted your heart at first sight. If you and your cat are to enjoy a long and happy future together, there are a number of factors that you will have to take into consideration before welcoming it into your home. Cats are increasingly living to ripe old ages – often up to twenty years – years during which you will have to be prepared to be a responsible owner. So before taking the plunge, ask yourself the following questions.

THIS MONTH-OLD KITTEN COULD NOTCH UP TWENTY YEARS.

Can I afford to keep a cat?

Although a cat's maintenance costs are relatively low, there are certain unavoidable expenses that cat-ownership will incur over the years. These include providing your feline with the minimum of two meals a day of a nutritious proprietary cat food; buying cat litter for an indoor cat; settling an annual veterinary bill for vaccinations; and funding any additional veterinary treatment that a cat may need as a result of an accident or illness. Investigate these costs by paying a visit to your local pet shop or supermarket and veterinary surgery, noting down prices and asking for information.

CAN YOU AFFORD TO FEED YOUR CAT A PROPRIETARY CAT FOOD TWICE A DAY?

Are my family circumstances suitable?

A cat's primary requirements are a regular supply of food and water, along with a safe and comfortable place of shelter: potentially your home. Can you guarantee to able to feed and water it every day, ideally twice a day, at the same time? Would your home suit the feline lifestyle? Although some cats do live in one-bedroom flats, most would prefer more space to roam around in, although a garden isn't necessary if you can supply alternative opportunities for exercise within your home. Despite the legendary feline independence, a cat will pine without some affection and attention – could you provide this if you are out working all day and partying at night? How would a cat fit in with any existing family members, children and other pets, for example? And what arrangements would you need to

THINK LONG AND HARD BEFORE WELCOMING A CAT INTO YOUR HOME.

make to ensure that it would be well looked after when you go away on holiday? Could you call on a neighbour to cat-sit, or would you need to arrange for it to stay in a cattery?

If, having considered these issues, you feel that you could give a cat a good home, there are still more decisions to be made.

Cat or kitten?

The essential question to ask yourself when deciding whether to adopt a cat or a kitten is whether you have sufficient time to devote to a young animal's needs. Although you should in any case never take a kitten from its mother before it has been weaned (usually when it is between eight and twelve weeks old), which makes feeding it easier, a kitten still requires a considerable amount of attention. Will you have the time to bond with it, to play with it (a vital part of kittenhood), to guide it as it becomes acquainted with its new household, to teach it human- and furniture-friendly habits, to rescue it from the scrapes that it will inevitably get itself into, and, above all, to make it feel a loved and valued member of your family?

LIKE ALL BABIES, KITTENS NEED LOTS OF AFFECTION AND ATTENTION.

VERY YOUNG KITTENS NEED THEIR MOTHER'S MILK.

There are also certain practical and financial considerations to be taken into account. You will probably have to take a kitten to the vet's for its first set of immunisation vaccinations (see pages 140 to 142), for example, and should also be prepared to foot the bill for medication, as well as provide nursing care, should it develop any ailments that you hadn't bargained for (in Caspar and Melchior's case, ear mites and ringworm). In addition, you may find yourself having to wean it from a diet to which it has become accustomed. All of these non-negotiable responsibilities take time and cost money. That having been said, kittens are fun-filled, captivating creatures, who are more tolerant of boisterous children than older cats, and it is fascinating to watch their personalities develop as they grow into adulthood. And when a cat has lived with you for most of its life, and you have years of shared companionship behind you, life simply wouldn't be the same without it.

Although it may require more patience to make it feel at home, adopting an older cat brings its own rewards. Certain aspects of its care will be easier: it will almost certainly be house-trained, for instance, and won't demand as much of your time and attention. The main difficulties will probably be educating it in the ways of your household and gently dissuading it from persisting with old habits – and you may even have to learn to live with them – as well as winning its trust and affection. If you persevere and forge a strong bond with it, however, even the most wary of adopted older cats will offer you their friendship, thereby enriching your life immeasurably.

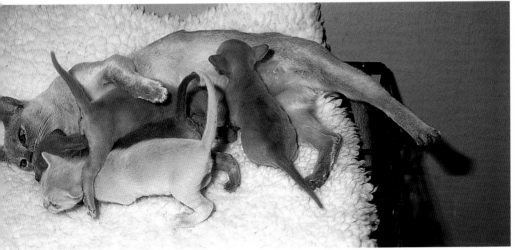

FEEDING TIME IS OFTEN A ROUGH-AND-TUMBLE AFFAIR WHEN KITTENS ARE INVOLVED.

KITTENS ARE BOTH CAPTIVATING . . .

. . . AND HIGHLY ENTERTAINING.

Male or female?

If, like the majority of responsible cat owners, you would prefer your cat not to breed, a simple neutering operation (see page 155) will iron out the most significant behavioural differences between male and female felines. With the removal of the organs that pump sex hormones – testosterone in males, and oestrogen in females – into the cat's body, both sexes will become less likely to roam or spray (particularly males), less temperamental and, most importantly, incapable of adding to an already teeming feline population. (Unchecked breeding has resulted in many unwanted kittens and cats, who, if they are lucky enough to survive in the first place, may be forced to become strays or to adopt a feral lifestyle.)

Unless you are prepared to keep, or find homes for, any kittens that she may have (and in her prime she may be capable of producing four or five three times a year), you should pre-empt the arrival of a litter of kittens by having any female cat that you adopt spayed as soon as your vet recommends it. Similarly, your male cat may sire numerous offspring – although the likelihood is that you'll be blissfully unaware of them – unless you take him to the vet to be castrated.

A SINGLE FEMALE WILL HAVE MANY OFFSPRING.

If, however, you would prefer your cat to remain entire, it's important that you're aware of the behavioural differences between male and female cats. A tom is unlikely to be at home much because his hormones will be urging him to patrol his territory to ward off trespassers, as well as to respond to the calls and scent of any local females on heat. In the laying-down of territorial markers, he will be an assiduous sprayer of pungent urine and may require frequent trips to the vet as a result of the wounds that he'll inevitably sustain in his scraps with other toms.

An entire female is usually more home-loving, apart from when she's on heat, when her sex hormones kick in and she'll begin to invite the attention of toms. If she becomes pregnant, her kittens will be born nine weeks later, her maternal duties then keeping her fully occupied for two to three months.

One cat or more?

The fact that we both went out to work during the day was at the forefront of our minds when we decided to adopt two kittens rather than one. When they are young, cats require a great deal of company and stimulation, and we felt that it would be unfair to leave a single kitten alone in our home for around ten hours a day during the working week. In this respect, letting ourselves in for double trouble was certainly the right decision for Caspar and Melchior, who, according to our downstairs neighbour, played a kitten's version of football all day while we were away. The downside is that keeping two cats well fed, healthy and happy does, of course, cost twice as much.

TWO CATS WILL PROVIDE COMPANY FOR EACH OTHER.

adopting a cat

When weighing up the pros and cons of how many cats to welcome into your home, you should first ask yourself what would be in the best interests of the cat or cats. Although cats are remarkably self-sufficient, a solitary kitten (but less so an older cat, who requires less active mutual interaction) could become lonely if it has to spend most of its time on its own. But if two are company, would three or more be too much of a crowd in a small home? Would you be able to provide each of your cats with sufficient food and a comfortable home, both of which top the list of cat priorities?

Don't forget to take your existing family into consideration, too. If your house is already packed with children, pets or both, how would they react to one or more cats joining them? Because it's far easier for kittens to learn to get along with both children and other household pets – even dogs – and vice versa, a single kitten would probably fit in better than either two or an older cat or cats. If you're tempted to adopt more than one kitten or cat, ask yourself whether it would be wise to take on the commitment of caring for them if space, time and money are already tight.

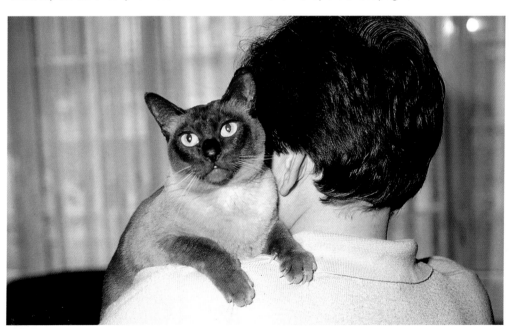

SITTING ON SHOULDER

A single cat is a good choice if you live on your own. Because you won't have to spread your attention thinly between two or more felines, the likelihood is that you'll forge a strong, companionable bond with your feline friend.

One or more? You'll probably already instinctively know the answer to that conundrum.

Moggie or pedigree?

Unless you intend to breed from, or show, your cat, there is little that a pedigree feline can offer that a mongrel moggie can't match. Just like people, every cat is a unique character, whether their lineage is uncertain or you can trace it back for many generations. Probably the only significant difference between purebreds like our Somali, Melchior, and crosspeds like his companion, Caspar, is that you can predict with reasonable accuracy how any kittens that a pedigree cat may have will look, especially if the other parent is of the same breed. And although it is often said that because moggies, unlike many pedigrees, aren't inbred, their mixed gene pool makes them more resistant to disease and generally tougher, this claim hasn't been scientifically substantiated (and in any case, many moggies are born into close-knit family groups).

EVEN SELF-SUFFICIENT CATS ENJOY SOCIAL INTERACTION.

89

When deciding whether to adopt a moggie or pedigree, the first consideration to be taken into account is cost. If you are charged for it at all – and many human surrogate parents of moggie kittens simply require the assurance that they will go to a good home – it is unlikely that you will be asked to pay more than a token sum for a crossped and, depending on its age, perhaps the cost of any initial immunisation vaccinations that it has been given. A carefully controlled parentage, on the other hand, commands a premium, and, depending on the breed, you may be asked to pay the equivalent of a washing machine or even a car for the privilege of becoming the owner of a purebred cat.

Both moggies and pedigrees come in a vast array of coat colours and fur lengths and, your personal preferences aside, you would be wise to take some of these into consideration. Cats with white coats, for example, are susceptible to sunburn and hence skin cancer, so, as ridiculous as it may sound, you should apply sunblock to their vulnerable noses and ears before allowing them outside to bask in the sunshine. Be warned, too, that white cats, especially if they have blue eyes, may be congenitally deaf. While longhaired cats often look magnificent, bear in mind that most will

need help with grooming and that you will therefore have to comb them regularly, often daily in the case of Persians. Their long, fine hairs may furthermore exacerbate an allergy to cat fur in humans, which may not be triggered by a shorthaired cat. Shorthairs usually manage to keep their coats sleek without human assistance, although it's still advisable to comb them once a week. All cats, be they long- or shorthairs, moult, so you should be prepared constantly to have to remove dead hairs from your clothing and furniture, but note that longhairs' soft awn hairs are particularly clingy (Melchior's light-silver fur, for example, seems to be magnetically attracted to dark clothing). Another disadvantage of owning a longhaired cat is that its self-grooming process can result in a build-up of fur in its stomach, resulting in the production of more furballs (see page 170) than in its shorthaired counterparts.

Despite every cat's individuality of personality, certain pedigree breeds are noted for their peculiarities of temperament. There follows a brief outline of a few pedigree personality types – if you are interested in learning more, consult a specialist guide and ideally also a breeder of the particular breed that appeals to you. Among the longhairs, Persians are typically easy-going,

LONGHAIRED CATS NEED HUMAN HELP TO KEEP THEIR MAGNIFICENT MANES TANGLE-FREE.

docile characters, as are the Ragdolls that are descended, the story goes, from a Persian female who had been injured in a road traffic accident. When handled, Ragdolls relax their bodies so that they become as floppy as the doll after which they are named, and it is also claimed that they have an extremely high pain threshold (which, of course, is no excuse to maltreat them).

Longhaired breeds that evolved from Oriental shorthairs tend to have retained the characteristics of their Oriental lineage. Being a

Somali (a longhaired Abyssinian), Melchior, for example, is a vocal, lively personality who is very human-oriented and likes to keep a constant eye on what we are doing, as well as join in phone conversations, in contrast to Caspar, our self-sufficient shorthaired crossped, who prefers to snooze the day away in peace.

British and European shorthaired breeds are usually quiet, even-tempered and relatively undemanding, unlike many of their Oriental shorthaired cousins, who are both incessant conversationalists and insist on playing an

FELINE CHARACTERISTICS CAN VARY GREATLY.

BRITISH SHORT HAIRED – RED SILVER SPOTTED

MAINE COON, RED, SILVER & WHITE

SNOWSHOE (MALE) SEAL AND WHITE POINT

active role in any household pursuit. Siamese and Burmese cats are especially renowned for their irrepressible curiosity and craving for close companionship and will frequently make their

own entertainment if left to their own devices (curtain-climbing is a particular favourite, as is wool-sucking). All in all, think hard about adopting a hyperactive feline!

ABYSSINIAN, BLUE

PERSIAN, BLUE TABBY

Cat sources

TINY KITTENS ARE VULNERABLE TO DISEASE.

Unless you have already reserved a kitten from the litter of a mother cat whose owner you know, your first port of call when looking for a cat to adopt should be your local vet's. Most veterinary surgeries display notice boards on which people whose cats have produced kittens, or those who sadly can no longer keep their older cats, can 'advertise' felines in need of a good home. Many veterinary nurses are in any case founts of knowledge and advice, both regarding reputable cat sources and aspects of feline care. Never buy a kitten from a pet shop: not only may it have been traumatised by its noisy surroundings, but it will in all likelihood have been exposed to a host of germs. And if a stray cat decides to adopt you, before giving it a permanent home, make every effort to ensure

that it is not already part of a loving family, particularly if it looks well fed.

A vet's notice board may also display the details of cat-rescue organisations, which is how, having first called to make an appointment, we found ourselves in the feline nursery of a suburban cat sanctuary where we were introduced to, among other kittens, Melchior and Caspar. Before making our choice, we were vetted to assess our suitability for cat-ownership and were also asked to sign an agreement undertaking to have the cats neutered; to take full responsibility for their welfare and to give them a happy and loving home; to obtain veterinary treatment in case of illness or injury; and to ensure that they wore identity tags when outside the home. In addition, we undertook to allow a member of the cat sanctuary to visit our home to check that the cats were happily settled; to return the cats to the sanctuary if we could no longer keep them; and, in the event of them going missing, to report their loss so that a search could be instigated. All of these stipulations had the cats' welfare at heart, and we were happy to go along with them, as well as make a modest donation towards the upkeep of the cat sanctuary.

Finally, if you are looking for a specific breed of pedigree cat, a good starting point is the pages of specialist cat magazines, which contain the contact details of societies and breeders.

REPUTABLE CAT SANCTUARIES TRY TO ENSURE THAT THEIR FELINE CHARGES GO TO GOOD HOMES.

95

What to look for in a kitten or cat

When meeting a prospective feline member of your family for the first time, be it a kitten or a cat, a crossped or a purebred, the essential question to ask yourself is whether it looks healthy. If you have any doubts, it would be wiser not to adopt it: not only could you be condemning yourself to exorbitant veterinary bills and a new career as a feline nurse, but you could even have to suffer the premature death of your feline charge.

In the case of kittens, remember that they should not leave their mother until they have been weaned, usually when they are between eight and twelve weeks old (although you can always reserve one earlier). If possible, ask to see the mother cat with her litter so that you can assess the cleanliness of their surroundings and also how the kittens interact, which should give you some idea of their respective personalities, as well as of their mother's temperament. Because you're likely to be charmed and distracted when you come face to face with a delightful heap of fluffy kittens, before leaving home it's best to write down a checklist of things to look out for to consult while carefully inspecting each kitten in turn.

A CAT'S EYES SHOULD BE CLEAR AND BRIGHT.

ASK TO SEE THE FELINE FAMILY INTERACTING.

The following checklist is as applicable in most respects to older cats as to kittens.

- Does the kitten look generally healthy and alert? If so, it has probably not contracted any life-endangering viruses or illnesses from its mother or environment.

- Any juvenile wobbliness aside, do the kitten's legs appear to be functioning normally? If it seems lame, it may be suffering from a non-reversible birth defect, have a broken limb or be showing the first signs of a serious illness.

- Do its ears look clean? Look out for head-shaking, ear-scratching, specks of dark grit or a profuse, brown, waxy discharge, all of which could be signs of ear mites (see page 204). These aren't disastrous, but the kitten's ears will need treating with eardrops to get rid of them.

- Do its eyes look clear and bright? Danger signs include soreness, weepiness, discharge and the third eyelid partially pulled across the eye, all of which indicate the presence of a potentially serious infection.

- Does its nose look clean and is it healthily damp? A runny nose may indicate cat flu (see page 144).

- Do its gums look rosy pink and its teeth white and healthy? Red, inflamed gums could be a sign of gingivitis (see pages 214 to 215) and pale ones a sign of illness.

- Is it sneezing, wheezing or coughing? All of these symptoms are potentially very serious.

- Does its fur look springy and in good condition? Are there any tiny black specks in it? A dirty, greasy, matted or bedraggled coat could indicate illness, and black specks a flea infestation (which, although not life-threatening, will require combating, see pages 149 to 151).

- Are there any bald spots in the fur? If so, the kitten, may have ringworm (see page 198), a fungal infection that will need to be treated with ointment and medication.

- Does it have a pronounced pot belly? If it does, it may be suffering from worms (see pages 146 to 148), which must be banished with medication.

- Does its bottom look clean? If you see any worms, these are relatively easily dealt with, but chronic-looking diarrhoea may a signify a grave illness.

On taking charge of Caspar and Melchior, the owner of the cat sanctuary warned us that they had ear mites (and Caspar must have been incubating ringworm, too, although there was no indication of that when we first met him). Both conditions cleared up completely after the appropriate treatment, but many of the

CURIOSITY IS A GOOD SIGN.

symptoms listed above may not be so easily dealt with. If you have any concerns, discuss them with the kitten's breeder or owner and don't allow your worries to be brushed aside. If you are really torn between what your head and heart – or the owner – are telling you, ask if you can take the kitten to a vet for an expert opinion; most responsible breeders or owners should have no objection to this, that is, as long as you pay the bill!

Personality-wise, look for friendly curiosity in a kitten. Some kittens may appear bossy and others more timid – you will know better than anyone else which personality traits will suit you and your home best, so be guided by your instincts, but nevertheless try to make an informed choice. Note that an older cat will often be a wary of strangers, so don't be put off if appears a little aloof.

Finally, remember that if a kitten or cat has been immunised you will need its vaccination certificate so that your vet knows which brand to use when it's time for its boosters. Along with a purebred, you should also be given a pedigree certificate stretching back four generations as proof of its lineage should you wish to show it or breed it with another pedigree.

Basic cat-care equipment

Before you welcome your cat or kitten into your home, you will need to prepare for its arrival by assembling the following cat-care basics.

A carrying basket

The first item that you'll need is a carrying basket in which to transfer your cat or kitten from its existing home to yours. Don't imagine that you will be able to carry it home in your arms: your feline is a creature of habit who will regard its previous place of residence as a safe haven, so as soon as you – after all, someone whom it doesn't know, and doesn't know means well – remove it from its familiar surroundings, it will panic and will start to lash out in an attempt to bolt away. If the feelings of high anxiety caused by its displacement weren't bad enough, it's more than likely that its journey to your home will necessitate an introduction to motorised transport, be it a car or a bus, the sounds and motion of which it will find so terrifyingly alien that it will freak out. The last thing you want is a frightened cat running amok under seats and foot pedals, so invest in a carrying basket, which you'll in any case need for future trips with your feline, such as to the veterinary surgery.

A CAT-CARRIER SHOULD BE WELL VENTILATED.

A BLANKET-LINED WICKER BASKET IS THE TRADITIONAL OPTION.

You'll find a selection of carrying baskets in your local pet shop, including traditional wicker baskets or fibreglass boxes with a grille-like front opening and plastic-covered, wire-mesh 'cages' that open at the top. Both types will do an efficient job of transporting a cat safely, but the wire-mesh carriers are probably more practical, being both more quickly cleaned should any panic-induced mishaps occur and easier to place a recalcitrant feline into (you can just drop them in, while you'll have to lift and push a cat into a front-opening carrier).

Whichever you choose, line the bottom with newspaper (or, after your cat has lost its fear and has become resigned to being incarcerated in its carrier, a piece of fabric), which will make the carrier more comfortable, as well as mopping up the mess if your petrified cat loses control of its bladder or bowels. If the weather's cold, line the sides with newspaper, too. Cardboard carriers may be cheaper, but they won't last long, and resist the temptation to place a cat in a zipped carrier or overnight bag – it simply won't give the cat enough air.

Food and dishes

In the interests of maintaining good hygiene, it's important that your cat has its own food and water bowls (separate ones are more practical than combined versions) rather than borrowing a saucer or dish from its human family. These are available from pet shops and should have a heavy base so that they won't tip over when your cat is eating or drinking. Battery-operated, covered food bowls are another option, many of which contain a type of cooling system that keeps food fresh in hot weather or over extended periods and may also incorporate a timer that you can set so that the lid springs open at a certain time when you're not around to feed your cat. If you have more than one cat, each should still be provided with its own pair of bowls to ensure that one doesn't hog them at feeding and watering times. (After their initial feeding frenzy, our cats tend to swap bowls midway through their meal, possibly, I suspect, to check whether they've been missing out on something more interesting.)

The best place to feed a cat is in the kitchen, where any spillages can be easily wiped away and bowls washed. A cat's sense of security is increased if it is always fed in the same spot, so pick a quiet corner where it can eat undisturbed by other members of your family and where you won't trip over its bowls. If the litter tray is also

situated in the kitchen (and, for the purposes of hygiene, try to keep it as far away from food-preparation areas as possible), it's best not to set the cat's bowls next to it as it will find the proximity of its food and lavatory most off-putting. If you – or your cat's – preferred food is fresh, tinned or semi-moist, its bowl should be washed after every meal, separately from the human family's dishes. Bowls that contain dried food can be washed less frequently, but

nevertheless at least once a week, along with water bowls. Use hot water and washing-up liquid to clean food and water bowls, but make sure that you rinse them thoroughly because the cat's sensitive noise doesn't find the smell of household detergents appetising.

You should change the water in your cat's water bowl twice a day (you'll find it easy to remember to do this if you get into the habit of

TO AVOID TEARS AT TEATIME, PROVIDE EACH CAT WITH ITS OWN FOOD BOWL.

emptying and refilling it just before feeding time). It's vital that a bowl of water is always available to your cat (this is especially crucial if you feed your cat dried food), but note that many cats won't drink from a freshly replenished water bowl until the smell of the chemicals with which the water has almost inevitably been treated has subsided to tolerable levels. Do not substitute milk for water: contrary to popular belief, cow's milk is not a feline staple (although many enjoy it) and, indeed, many cats find the lactose that it contains difficult to digest, the result being diarrhoea.

MILK GIVES SOME CATS DIARRHOEA.

What, and when, should you feed your feline?

ITS MOTHER'S MILK PROVIDES ALL OF THE NOURISHMENT THAT A YOUNG KITTEN NEEDS.

The first thing to note is that a cat's nutritional requirements will change throughout the course of its life. Their mother's milk contains all of the nutrients that kittens need for the first month or two of their lives, after which, in the wild, they would be weaned on mice and other sources of fresh flesh. Your kitten should have been weaned before it moves in with you, but because its nose and stomach will probably have become accustomed to a particular diet, you will probably have to wean it off this gradually before switching to your preferred alternative full-time. Remember to ask its previous owner for details of what it's been used to eating (this precaution also applies to older cats, who dislike change), and, if necessary, a diet sheet. Just like human babies, kittens have small stomachs and will therefore need to be fed more often than adult cats, so aim to give them four small meals a day. By the time that your cat is six months old, you should have reduced its meals to two a day (one in the morning and one in the evening), thereby instituting a feeding regime that will remain the same for the rest of its life, that is, as long as it remains healthy. Your vet will be able to advise you when, and what, to feed an ill, convalescent or old cat, but see also pages 164 to 166.

Gone are the days when domestic cats procured their own food, supplemented by a few scraps from their household's kitchen. And although you can certainly give your cat the occasional treat of a morsel of cooked fish, meat or poultry or cheese (see pages 164 to 165) to spice up its diet, providing it exclusively with home-cooked food, day in, day out, is not only extremely impractical, but could also result in your cat's body becoming deficient in some of the essential nutrients that are vital for the maintenance of feline health. Just as the make-up of a cat's body is specific to a cat, so its body needs the correct balance of feline-fuelling nutrients to avoid malnourishment and to enable every part of its body to function efficiently. The bodies, and hence nutritional needs, of human omnivores, as well as of dogs, differ from those of felines, so don't think that a

TINNED CAT FOOD

PACKET CAT FOOD

DRY CAT FOOD WITH WATER

cat will thrive on a human or canine diet – it won't. Protein, for example, which is required to maintain organs, muscles and tissues, should make up 30 to 40 per cent of a cat's diet, around three times the level recommended for a dog, and it also needs fat (at least 10 to 15 per cent) for energy, along with fibre (around 7 per cent) for roughage and trace amounts of vitamins and minerals.

To ensure that your kitten or cat consumes all of the nutrients that it needs, and thus remains fit and healthy, the safest option is to base its diet on a 'complete' (not 'complementary', 'treat', 'incomplete', 'varietal' or any similar euphemism, so check the label carefully) proprietary cat food, be it tinned, foil-packed or dry. You'll then be secure in the knowledge that the cat-food industry's experts in feline nutrition

MOST PROPRIETARY CAT FOODS HAVE BEEN FORMULATED TO MEET A FELINE'S NUTRITIONAL NEEDS.

KITTENS SHOULD BE WEANED WHEN THEY ARE BETWEEN EIGHT AND TWELVE WEEKS OLD.

have ensured that their products contain exactly the right proportions of the nutrients that are essential for the maintenance of feline health. Some cats find tinned or foil-packed food more appetising than dry, although the disadvantages to humans include their powerful smell and speedy rate of spoilage. Dry food generally works out cheaper than its tinned or foil-packed counterparts and has the further advantage of offering less wastage, also giving the cat's teeth

and gums a thorough work-out (remember that feline teeth were designed to crunch on bones). Most reputable manufacturers of cat food offer a range of products that have been specially formulated to suit every cat's age and condition, and their labels usually contain guidelines advising you how much of the product to feed your cat a day. If you have any doubts about what, and when, to feed your feline, ask your vet for advice.

YOU'LL NEED A LITTER SCOOP ...

A litter tray and its accoutrements

Even if your new feline is going to be an outdoor cat, you'll still need to buy a litter tray for it to use while it settles into your household, when you should keep it house-bound until you are certain that knows where home is (see page 129). Once you have given it permission to roam, your cat will regard your garden as a giant litter tray, but there will nevertheless be occasions when you'll have to resurrect the real thing: if your cat becomes ill and can't stray too far from its sickbed, for example, or if you have to disbar it from going outside for a day or two. A litter tray is essential for indoor cats, along with cat litter and a litter scoop with which to carry out ad hoc waste removal. See page 168 for details on how often to change cat litter and

clean a litter tray. Visit your pet shop to see what kind of litter trays, cat litter and scoops they stock. Basic litter trays consist of a shallow, toughened-plastic tray, but if you can afford it I'd recommend that you buy a covered one (the lid is easily detachable for cleaning the tray) because it gives the user more privacy and also limits the amount of cat litter that inevitably ends up being scattered around the floor. Some covered litter trays incorporate a cat-flap-type swing door, but many suspicious cats (ours included) refuse to enter this lavatorial portal.

You'll also need cat litter, and if your cat or kitten is already trained to use a litter tray, remember to ask its breeder or owner which

...A LITTER TRAY AND CAT LITTER.

A COVERED LITTER TRAY GIVES A LITTLE PRIVACY.

of a large plant pot. Flummoxed, we contacted the owner of the cat sanctuary for advice, and it transpired that they'd been used to a granule-type litter, whereas we'd provided them with an alien, fuller's-earth-based product. The litter was changed and the problem was solved.

If they aren't already familiar with a litter tray, most kittens and cats instinctively understand their purpose and need only to be shown its location, although as an educative measure you could always lift your feline into the tray, gently hold its front paws and then make a scratching motion with them.

type of litter it has been used to. We neglected to do this, and although we'd shown the new arrivals the litter tray, they weren't keen to enter it, after a day of leg-crossing finally leaving a deposit or two overnight on the earthy surface

CATS UNDERSTAND THE LITTER-TRAY CONCEPT.

Equipment for the indoor and outdoor cat

A CAT FLAP WILL GIVE YOUR CAT INDEPENDENCE.

If you intend your feline to be an outdoor cat, think about how it is going to gain access to the great outdoors.

With your special skill as a door-opener, are you prepared to be miaowed at every time, day or night, that your cat wants to be let in or out? If not, and you don't want to restrict your cat's movements, fitting a cat flap into a wall or door (for which some DIY expertise will be required) is probably the answer. Many types of cat flap are sold by pet shops, all of which operate on

WHEN INSTALLING A CAT FLAP, REMEMBER TO POSITION

the hinged-flap principle, with most featuring a catch that shuts the flap should you wish to keep your cat inside. Some variants are magnet-operated, with a magnet in the cat flap whose polarity corresponds to one that the cat

ENDLY HEIGHT.

PROVIDE AN INDOOR CAT WITH A SCRATCHING POST.

TAKE STEPS TO SAFEGUARD YOUR FURNITURE.

wears on its collar, giving it its personal pass key and preventing strange cats from invading the house. For easy feline access, a cat flap should be situated no higher than 6 centimetres (around 2½ inches) above ground level.

Outdoor cats can strop their claws on fences and trees, but unless you provide an indoor cat with a scratching post, it will be forced to turn its attention to your cherished furniture. Your options are either to improvise, by, perhaps, giving your cat a log of wood (one that won't splinter) to scratch at, or to buy a scratching post (or a wall-mounted scratching panel) from a pet shop. Most consist of a wooden pole around which rope is tightly coiled, fixed into a wooden base that is usually covered with carpet fabric (which I personally think may confuse a cat: if it's encouraged to scratch the base of the scratching post, why not also your expensive Axminster?) Some incorporate a horizontal spur from which a ball on a string dangles, temptingly inviting play, and others support a platform on the top (ideal for kittens to leap on in play, although there is a risk that an older cat's weight won't be spread across it evenly, causing the apparatus to topple over). Note that a scratching post will become well worn from constant use and will therefore eventually have to be replaced, and also that when your cat is adult a scratching post should be as tall as possible to enable your feline to stretch up to enhance the stropping experience.

Finally, although theories vary as to why, all cats like to eat grass. In the absence of the real thing, an indoor cat may nibble at a house plant (which could poison it, see page 124), so be a considerate owner and grow it a pot of indoor grass; grass seeds specifically recommended for feline consumption are stocked by many gardening outlets.

OPINION VARIES AS TO WHY FELINES NIBBLE AT GRASS AND FOLIAGE, BUT THEY DO.

Grooming equipment

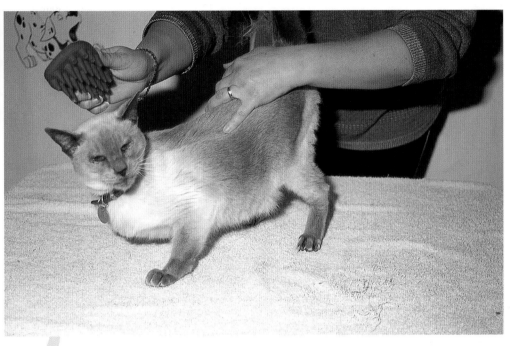

PET SHOPS STOCK MANY FELINE GROOMING AIDS, AND, IF NOTHING ELSE, AT LEAST INVEST IN A CAT COMB.

Unless you are about to become the proud owner of a Sphynx, which has no hair at all, if you buy nothing else in the way of grooming equipment, you should at least invest in a comb that has been specially designed for felines (not a human one) to help your cat to keep its coat tangle-free. Human-assisted grooming is vital for longhaired cats to prevent their coats from becoming so drastically matted that the only solution is a trip to the vet's to have the solid clumps of fur shaved away. Grooming your cat will lessen the frequency with which it vomits up furballs, too, as well as giving you the opportunity regularly to check for fleas and skin problems. Two types of cat comb are typically sold by pet shops: ones with short teeth of identical length for shorthairs and others with long teeth interspersed with shorter ones for longhairs. Both normally have plastic handles with fingerholds moulded into them to give the

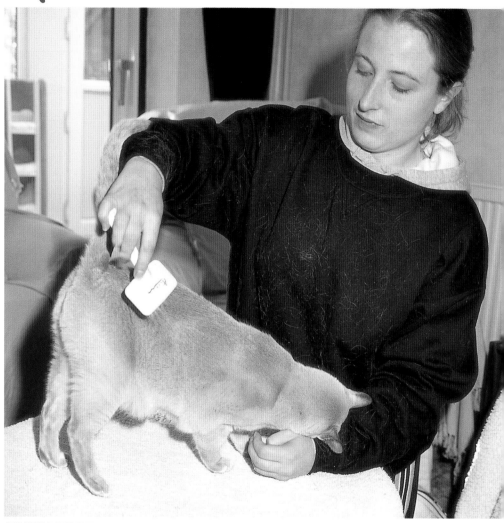

GROOMING PROVIDES AN OPPORTUNITY FOR YOU TO BOND WITH YOUR CAT.

human groomer a good grip. In addition, if you are anticipating the arrival of a longhaired feline, you may like to invest in a soft-bristled cat brush with which to give your cat's coat a final smoothing, while an old toothbrush is ideal for brushing its facial fur. (See pages 169 to 172 for guidance on how to groom both long- and shorthaired cats.)

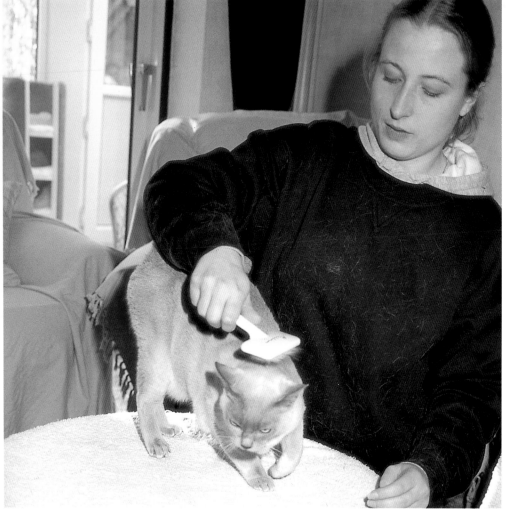

AS A FINISHING TOUCH, YOU COULD USE A SLICKER BRUSH TO GIVE YOUR CAT'S COAT A GLOSSY SHEEN.

Claw-clippers are usually a prerequisite for an indoor cat, who, unlike a freely wandering feline, will not have the opportunity to keep its front claws in trim (although it will pull off its back claws with its incisor teeth once they have outlived their usefulness) by walking on hard surfaces or stropping them against wooden objects. Even if you provide your indoor cat with

a scratching post, it still may not indulge in regular enough stropping sessions to shorten its claws adequately, which is when a human wielding a pair of clippers – either ones designed specifically for felines or human toenail-clippers – should step in to provide assistance. (See pages 172 to 173 on how to cut your cat's claws.)

MANY CATS ENJOY THE SENSATION OF BEING MASSAGED AS THEY ARE BEING GROOMED.

Finally, consult your vet about maintaining your feline's dental health. Depending on your cat's age and diet, you may be advised to clean its teeth regularly, using a plastic finger brush and toothpaste that has been specially formulated for cats (human toothpaste is unsuitable). Although you may scoff at the notion, the alternative may be that your cat's teeth become decayed (having paid a vast sum to have two of Melchior's teeth extracted by the vet under general anaesthetic, I have now become an assiduous brusher of our cats' teeth).

CAT TOOTH BRUSHES

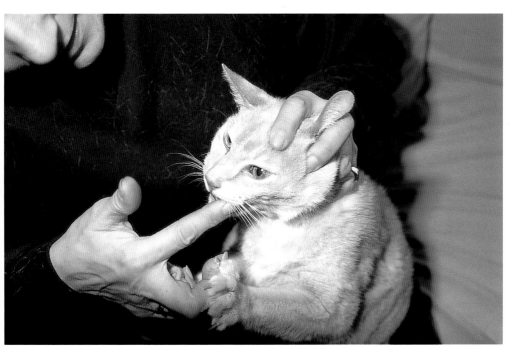

YOU'D BE ADVISED TO CLEAN YOUR CAT'S TEETH, BUT MAY PREFER TO USE A FINGER BRUSH.

117

A PLASTIC CAT BED HAS THE ADVANTAGE OF BEING EASY TO CLEAN.

A cat bed

Unless you welcome the idea of sharing your bed with your cat and suffering the consequences in terms of sleep-deprivation (a cat will rarely stay co-operatively prone at the bottom of the bed all night), start as you mean to go on and prepare a bed for it. The day on which it arrives in its new home will be bewildering and tiring for your kitten or cat, and after the adrenaline rush has subsided it will welcome a comfortable bed in which to sleep to enable it to recover from the upheaval that it has experienced.

Pet shops stock an array of feline beds, from traditional wicker baskets to washable oversized cushions and bean-bags to fake-fur nests and igloos. If you buy a basket-type bed, your comfort-loving cat will appreciate some extra padding and insulation in the form of an old blanket, which should be washed regularly, just

A KITTEN'S FIRST BED

PROVIDE YOUR CAT WITH SOME EXTRA INSULATION.

as the bed itself should be kept clean. A cheaper provisional alternative is to make a cat bed from a sturdy cardboard box by cutting off any flaps, placing it on its base (cut out a section at the front to act as a doorway) or side and lining it with newspaper topped with a blanket. As an extra welcoming touch, particularly for a kitten, who may miss its mother and littermates' body heat, you could slip an electric heating pad (for safety's sake, one designed specially for felines) or hot-water bottle filled with warm, but not boiling, water under the blanket, but place it at the side, rather than centrally, so that the cat has a choice of a warm or cold spot to curl up on.

Think carefully about where to place your prospective feline's bed: you may be tempted to position it at the hub of family life so that it feels included and you can continue to admire it while it sleeps, but this will probably not suit the

cat's need to feel private and safe when it abandons itself to unconsciousness. It is usually better to position the bed in a quiet corner where it can sleep undisturbed. In addition, try to choose a draught-free spot so that your cat won't become chilly – test for cat-level draughts by getting down on your hands and knees – and if this is by a radiator or gets some sun during the day, so much the better: cats adore luxuriating in comforting warmth as they sleep.

Be warned, however, that as your cat gains in confidence, it may ignore the bed that you have so considerately provided, instead preferring a snoozing place of its own choice, such as an armchair or your own bed.

A BED WILL MAKE YOUR CAT FEEL MORE AT HOME.

119

Toys for feline girls and boys

ENSURE THAT A MOUSE'S 'EYES' ARE FIRMLY ATTACHED.

If you are bringing home a kitten, it is important that you provide it with some toys to play with: play is a vital part of a kitten's development, whereby it practises its chasing and pouncing skills. Playing with your kitten will also strengthen the bond between you, as well as being great fun for all of the game's participants, be they human or feline. The imaginations of older cats, too, are often stimulated by a toy mouse to 'hunt', particularly if they are indoor cats who neither have access to the real thing nor much opportunity to exercise. Although, for example, our pair of twelve-year-olds have reached the age when they no longer always spring into action when a thing-on-a-string is dangled in front of their noses, toy mice materialise overnight in spots where once there were none, evidence that our felines are not too old to indulge in nocturnal games of cat and mouse.

The manufacturers of cat toys are constantly supplying pet shops with ever-more ingenious products, from mice on strings and springs to balls containing bells. Many fabric mice are stuffed with dried catnip (*Nepeta cataria*), a plant that sends many cats into paroxysms of ecstasy, making such mice irresistibly attractive playthings. There's no need to spend money on your feline's entertainment, however: a table-tennis ball will provide many fun-packed sessions of high-octane exercise and excitement, as will a crumpled-up paper bag, while a cotton reel tied to a piece of string – with you attached to the other end to jerk it into action and pull around – for your cat to stalk and pounce on will provide it with all of the exhilarating thrill of the chase.

Before introducing any new toy to your cat, first ensure that it is an object with which a cat can safely play. Make sure that any mouse 'eyes', for example, are securely attached, that there are no protruding pins or staples that could cause injury, that a rubber toy isn't small enough to be swallowed and also be vigilant about preventing your cat from ingesting lengths of string or wool. Note, too, that most cats are terrified, rather than intrigued by, clockwork or motorised toys.

HUMAN–FELINE GAMES ARE GREAT FUN.

TOYS PROVIDE SENSORY STIMULATION.

NOTHING IS SACRED AT PLAYTIME.

PLAY PROVIDES HUNTING PRACTICE.

Making your home safe for your cat

Within a few hours of his arrival in his new home, Caspar the kitten went missing. Certain that he couldn't have ventured outside, but baffled as to what sort of hiding place he could have found in a modestly sized flat, we searched high and low, to no avail. Something eventually led us into the kitchen, and then to the upright fridge–freezer. There was a small gap between the back of the appliance and the wall . . . he couldn't have, could he? Sure enough, on pulling out the unit, we discovered our new kitten curled up in a space within the backless freezer, its electrical innards all the while buzzing away ominously. This cautionary tale goes to show that you should take the same stringent precautions to make your home safe for a new kitten or cat that you would for a toddler – even more so, since toddlers lack the advanced escapology skills of a cat.

The tale of Caspar the kitten also highlights the advisability of introducing a kitten or cat to only one room of your home for the first day or so, although this strategy may not always be practical if its food and water bowls, as well as its litter tray, are in a different room. However many rooms you decide to give your new feline access to on its arrival, you should at least pre-empt it streaking off through windows and doors by making sure that they are firmly shut. Another chapter from the annals of Caspar's kittenhood tells of how he managed to push up, by squeezing under, a first-floor sash window that was open at the bottom by about an inch. Having startled him as he was sitting on the windowsill enjoying the view, he reacted by leaping down into the garden, 5 metres (around 16 feet) below. Thankfully, apart from everyone

AN OPEN WINDOW: AN OPPORTUNITY TO ESCAPE?

ELECTRICAL APPLIANCES AND THREAD SPELL 'DANGER'!

concerned having had a fright, no damage was done, but many cats who suffer similar falls are not so lucky: because they may have been snoozing peacefully when they slipped off a windowsill, they may not be able to alert their senses in time to ensure that they land on their feet. Alternatively, even if they manage to land on all four paws, the force of their impact on landing may be so great that their legs buckle and break and their jaw may hit the ground and be smashed. It's therefore crucial that you're especially vigilant about your cat's safety if you live in a high-rise flat or if your home has a balcony and, if your cat persists on sleeping on a windowsill, it would be wise to fit some sort of barrier – perhaps a trellis – along it to prevent a fall.

Because it is not unusual for panicked kittens to shoot up fireplaces, if there are any open ones in your house, either place a fireguard around them or stuff the chimney flues with newspaper. In addition, try to tuck any trailing electrical cables out of the way of a cat, who may be tempted to exercise its teeth and gums by gnawing on them. When it is feeling brave enough to explore every inch of your home, a kitten in particular will leap onto any available surface, so it would be sensible to take the precaution of temporarily stowing any breakable objects, such as vases, out of harm's way. Don't leave threaded sewing needles where a cat could gain access to them either: it could be tempted to chew, or play with, the dangling

BLOCK YOUR CAT'S ACCESS TO AN OPEN FIREPLACE.

thread, presenting the very real danger that it may swallow the needle; rubber bands can also wreak internal havoc if ingested. Remember, too, that a decorated Christmas tree represents a challenging activity centre to a cat. Speaking from rueful experience, unless you shut the door on your Christmas tree at night, you may wake up to a scene of devastation, with glass decorations smashed to smithereens (and a cat with bleeding feet), sodden piles of regurgitated lametta strewn all over the floor and possibly also widespread damage caused by a toppled tree.

MANY SUBSTANCES PRESENT A DANGER TO YOUR CAT.

Try to scrutinise your kitchen from your cat's vantage point: if a saucepan or kettle boils over, for example, your feline could be splashed and scalded by the boiling liquid. Another danger to cats lies in common household chemicals like bleach, which could burn or poison them, so keep them out of your cat's way, preferably in a cupboard. The same goes for any caustic or corrosive liquids, such as paint-thinners, paraffin, creosote and pesticides. But be warned: although he cannot rival Caspar's talent for getting himself into hair-raising scrapes, the ever-inquisitive Melchior has perfected the art of opening the doors of certain cupboards with his paw and nose, so make sure that any cupboards which you don't want your cat rooting around in have firmly sprung hinges or magnetic catches and always keep the doors of washing machines and tumble-driers shut.

Note, too, that certain plants, including mistletoe, ivy, poinsettia, rhododendrons and azaleas, oleander, *Philodendron*, *Caladium*, *Dieffenbachia*, *Prunus laurocerasus* and *Solanum capiscastrum*, can poison cats, so don't grow any of these inside and reduce the risk of a house plant being nibbled by providing an indoor cat with its own pot of grass (see page 112).

The big day: bringing your cat home

As the great day dawns, you'll awake to the realisation that life will never be quite the same again. Ideally, you will have arranged to collect your cat or kitten on a day when you will be at home so that you can reassure it and get to know each other, and also when your household will be as quiet as possible. Before collecting the new feline addition to the family, check that you have all of the food and equipment that you'll need to take care of your cat and also that you have positioned its food and water bowls, bed and litter tray in suitable spots – as a temporary measure, perhaps in the room to which you'll first introduce it (when your

A HEATED BED ESPECIALLY DESIGNED FOR FELINES.

cat feels at home, you can move them to more permanent places). Finally, before picking up your cat-carrier (don't forget to line it with newspaper) and heading out through the door, ensure that all doors and windows are firmly shut.

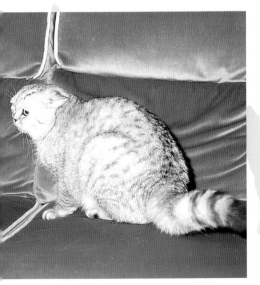

YOUR NEW CAT WILL INEVITABLY BE FRIGHTENED.

INTRODUCE IT TO ITS BED TO MAKE IT FEEL AT HOME.

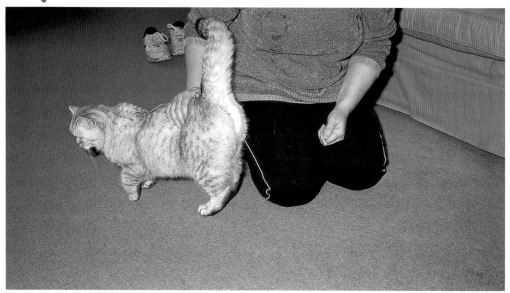

STROKING THE NEW ARRIVAL WILL REASSURE IT, BUT WAIT FOR YOUR NEW-FOUND FRIEND TO APPROACH YOU FIRST.

AFTER A DAY OF UPSET AND UPHEAVAL, YOUR CAT MAY BE IN NEED OF SOME REST AND RECUPERATON.

On coming face to face with your kitten or cat for the first time on your mutual big day, don't abruptly bundle it into its carrier: spare a few minutes to give it some attention so that it knows that your intentions are friendly, and also be patient as its previous owner bids it farewell. Remember to ask for any tips, for example, regarding the diet or type of cat litter that it's been used to, and only then lift your cat gently into its carrying basket. As you wend your way home together, make soothing noises in response to any terrified yowls that your cat may make to express its fear at being torn away from the safety of its home by a stranger – it will inevitably be terrified, particularly if it's enduring a close encounter with a car for the first time. Do not, however, under any circumstance, be tempted to remove it from its carrier to stroke or cuddle it: the best-case scenario is that chaos will ensue.

YOU'LL TERRIFY YOUR ALREADY TRAUMATISED CAT IF YOU MAKE A LUNGE FOR IT.

Once you have arrived home, set the cat's carrier in the room that you've temporarily allotted your cat and don't let it out until you have taken off your coat, have shut the door and are ready to give it your undivided attention as it takes its first tentative steps out of its basket and into its new home. Give it some words of gentle encouragement, but don't make a lunge for it to give it a reassuring cuddle, which would only scare it. Instead, sit back and let it explore its new surroundings. If, as is likely, it either slinks or bolts to a spot that offers it cover and a sense of security, such as behind the sofa, don't attempt to haul it out, just wait until its curiosity prevails and it's plucked up the courage to venture out again. Watch patiently as it explores the room and, when it feels confident enough to approach you, offer it a caressing stroke, but don't make any sudden movements. If it hasn't already discovered them, and when you have

WHEN YOUR CAT STARTS TO FEEL AT HOME, ITS CURIOSITY WILL PREVAIL.

built up sufficient trust between you to enable you to pick it up (see pages 130 to 131 for how to handle it), take it to its litter tray and water bowl – it may be very relieved to make their acquaintance – followed by its bed.

Don't feed your cat until you are certain that it is starting to feel at home (a good sign is when it starts washing itself, which indicates that it's feeling relatively relaxed). Thereafter, if both of you are still up to it, you could introduce it to the rest of the house – but not to the garden – taking your time to allow it to investigate each room in turn, a process that, depending on the size of your home, it may be sensible to stretch out over some days. Don't leave it to its own devices, but shadow it to ensure that it doesn't bolt – or creep inside a fridge-freezer! Finally, exploration complete, return to the room from which you started out together, which it should by now regard as the core of its new home.

At a kitten's bedtime, tucking a hot-water bottle or heated pad (see page 119) under one side of its bedding for the first few nights of its residency will provide some reassuring, sleep-inducing warmth (older cats may appreciate this, too). Some people also advocate placing a clockwork alarm clock near it – but make sure that the alarm's switched off – to simulate the familiar rhythm of its mother's heartbeat.

Whatever your new cat's age, it's best not to give it access to the great outdoors for at least a week (and in the case of nervous felines, three) to give it the opportunity to become thoroughly familiar with its home, to which it should then always return, if only at feeding time!

Handling your cat

Cats admittedly have loose skins, but unless your feline is a kitten whose mother has, until very recently, picked it up by the scruff of its neck – and even she will have found it increasingly difficult as it gained weight – don't attempt this. Although grasping the scruff of the neck can, in emergencies (see page 248), trigger a reflex reaction that causes the cat to freeze, a kitten or cat should never be lifted in this way because its skin will simply not be able to bear the cat's weight.

Before picking up your cat, try to ensure that it is relaxed – ideally, approach it slowly, all the while talking to it quietly – and never make a grab for it. The correct way in which to pick up an acquiescent cat who is standing on the ground is to slip one hand under its chest, just behind its front legs, and then, using a scooping motion, gently to push its back legs forward with the other hand, before lifting the cat until it is level with your waist. In this way, between them your hands will both be supporting your feline's entire weight and

THE CORRECT WAY TO HOLD A CAT, WITH BOTH HANDS SUPPORTING ITS ENTIRE WEIGHT.

making it feel as secure and comfortable as possible. An alternative method that is often used by judges at cat shows is to hold the cat's front legs with one hand and to place the other under its abdomen before carefully lifting the feline for inspection.

Never cradle a cat across your chest with its abdomen and face pointing upwards, as you would a baby, because this position will make it feel vulnerable and will also cause its back to slump awkwardly. Instead, slightly modify your lifting technique so that the cat is upright, with its face and body pointing outwards, in the same direction as yours, with its weight supported by one hand cupped under its hindquarters (you may find it easier to settle it in the crook of your arm) and the other lightly, but firmly, encircling its chest, again under the forelegs. Because some cats do not take kindly to being restrained in this way, however lovingly, the outward-pointing position has the advantage of ensuring that your face is not the first target of an irritable cat's claws.

Talking to it soothingly as you are holding your feline will reassure it of your friendly intentions, helping to settle it.

A KITTEN'S BONES ARE FRAGILE, SO NEVER SQUEEZE IT TIGHTLY LEST YOU BREAK THEM.

Your cat and children

A HARMONIOUS FELINE–HUMAN FAMILY.

could end up being badly scratched as the infuriated cat tries to escape its well-meaning tormentor. Be warned that if a cat suffers consistent mishandling by children, it could develop either exaggeratedly aggressive or timid self-defensive behavioural patterns.

Kittens, who will not be able to resist the lure of a game for long, will usually get on better with a child than an older, more self-contained cat, who will be set in its ways. Even so, try as best you can to explain to your youngster that a kitten can easily be injured, that it needs to be left in peace to sleep when it is tired and that its tail is not a plaything. Although the feline nature is markedly different to ours, it may be expedient to humanise your cat when laying down feline-friendly laws to a young child: for example, 'You know how cross you feel when you're tired? Well the kitten feels just the same, so let's leave it alone for a while to have a sleep and you can play with it later'. In the case of older children, involving them in aspects of your cat's care will give them a sense of proud responsibility, but be vigilant about your feline's welfare and never delegate its overall care to them – assume a supervisory, if hands-off, role instead.

Teaching a child how to handle a cat correctly will ensure the safety of both, but may be difficult to drum into young children, who will probably be beside themselves with excitement at the arrival of a feline playmate. (And it's kinder to the new cat to arrange for them to be out of the house when you first introduce it to your home.) In fact, it's best to discourage children under the age of six from picking up your cat at all: kittens' bones are still relatively soft and fragile, and an overly enthusiastic hug from a child could easily cause a fracture, while a small child will certainly not be able to bear the weight of an older cat, and in any case

CHILDREN AND KITTENS ARE UNITED IN THEIR LOVE OF PLAYTIME, BUT ALWAYS ENSURE A KITTEN'S SAFETY.

Finally, there are certain rules that you must abide by if cats and children share the same house.

● Never leave a sleeping baby where a cat could sit on it: the cat will be attracted by the baby's warmth and could inadvertently smother it.

● In the interests of maintaining both your child and your cat's health, discourage your child from human–feline face-rubbing, allow neither access to the other's food and, most importantly, ensure that your child stays away from the cat's litter tray to avoid the risk of toxoplasmosis infection (see page 168).

TEACH YOUR CHILD TO RESPECT THE FAMILY CAT.

Your cat and other household pets

Felines and many other species of household pet will mix well, but only in certain circumstances. A cat will instinctively regard anything smaller than itself as potential prey, a viewpoint that will not change with familiarisation, so make sure that the aquaria of fish and the cages of mice, hamsters and birds, for instance, are cat-proof or you may end up with a massacre on your hands. A kitten will generally fit in well with a household's existing cats and dogs, in whom it may arouse protective instincts. In the case of an existing cat, a kitten will either be tolerated or ignored, while a dog will usually eventually develop an affectionate *modus vivendi* with it, even if, as

CATS WILL OFTEN RUB ALONG QUITE WELL TOGETHER.

DOGS AND CATS USUALLY LEARN TO LIVE TOGETHER.

EATING TOGETHER SIGNIFIES MUTUAL ACCEPTANCE.

usually occurs, the kitten ends up ruling the roost. Difficulties may, however, arise if an older cat is introduced to a household that already includes an adult feline or canine, which will typically regard the new arrival as a threat to the established order. Being inevitably wary, the new cat will probably avoid contact with it, and if it has had bad experiences with dogs in particular, a bond will never be formed. And the smaller the dog, the harder co-existence will be, since the natural status quo determined by size will be blurred.

The introduction of a feline 'intruder' into a household that includes other pets will initially be fraught, involving much growling, hissing, spitting and posturing, but with time, patience and the use of certain strategies, your pets should eventually come to tolerate, if not enjoy, each other's presence in your – their – home.

- Keep existing pets away from the new arrival by shutting them in another room until you have had the time to acquaint it properly with both yourself and your home.

- Because a shared, 'family' smell is of crucial importance to both cats and dogs' sense of security, during the separation period place a blanket or cushion that one has been sitting on in the other's domain to familiarise each

with the other's personal odour. This should firstly mean that when they finally come face to face the other won't seem so alien and, secondly, that the other's signature scent will come to be identified over time as a vital element of their home's overall smell.

- Supervise your respective pets' introduction to each other (keep a dog on a lead) and do not leave them alone together (again, segregate them in separate rooms) for at least a few weeks, until you are sure that they have grudgingly accepted each other and are unlikely to fight.

- Feed them in different parts of your home. It may take two or more weeks until they are relaxed enough with each other to eat together, and even thereafter don't force them to share the same food bowl.

- Divide your attention between each of them equally: although the feline newcomer needs to feel reassured, you may fuel your existing pet's resentment if it is made to feel that its position in your affections has been usurped by the recent arrival.

3

Cat-care
fundamentals

Registering with a vet

Cats that enjoy being bundled into their carriers and whisked to a strange-smelling examining room to suffer the indignity of being inspected from head to tail are few and far between, but a regular trip to the vet's is nevertheless a necessary evil if your cat is to remain healthy.

If you didn't have it examined before adopting it, it's crucial that you make an appointment with your vet within a few days of having taken charge of your new kitten or cat. It's only a vet's experienced eye that will detect the first signs of either a life-threatening illness or a troublesome ailment, both of which must be treated as soon as possible. If you leave it too long, by the time that some innocuous signs have become full-blown symptoms, it may be too late to save the life of a feline who is rapidly becoming a fast friend.

A thorough check-up is not the only reason why a cat should be registered with a veterinary surgery as soon as you can arrange it: a kitten must have its first vaccinations against certain life-threatening, feline-specific diseases (see pages 140 to 145), while an older cat must have annual booster injections to maintain the immunity that previous vaccinations have given it. The correct timing of these vaccinations is of the essence, otherwise there will be a window of

opportunity for these serious viruses to take hold when the feline's immune system is powerless to fight them off. Vaccination time is furthermore a good opportunity for the vet to check your cat's overall health and to give it a precautionary worming pill. Regular feline and veterinary get-togethers will also give you the chance to ask your vet's advice about any niggling concerns that you may have about your cat's health, dietary regime or behavioural quirks.

Although there is no state-supported health-care system for cats, financial concerns should never prevent your cat from receiving the veterinary attention that it needs, so consider spreading the cost of any future treatment by taking out an insurance policy (your vet will provide you with the details of health-insurance companies for pets, but note that these do not cover routine care). Remember, too, that certain animal-welfare organisations will treat a sick cat for either no charge or a minimal cost.

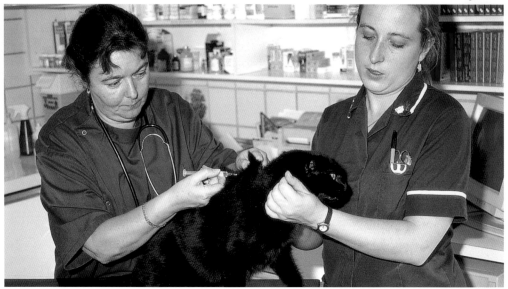

KITTENS AND CATS MUST BE REGULARLY VACCINATED AGAINST CAT-KILLING DISEASES.

ONLY A VET'S EXPERIENCED EYE CAN IDENTIFY SOME SIGNS THAT ALL IS NOT WELL.

Vital vaccinations

There are three viral diseases against which you must immunise your kitten or cat: feline panleucopenia, feline infectious respiratory disease and feline leukaemia, all of which are easily spread and potentially fatal to a cat who hasn't been vaccinated against them.

Indeed, the key to whether or not your cat's immune system will be able to battle these highly infectious viruses successfully, should it come into contact with them at any time from birth to old age, is found in the form of a hypodermic needle and a phial of the appropriate vaccine.

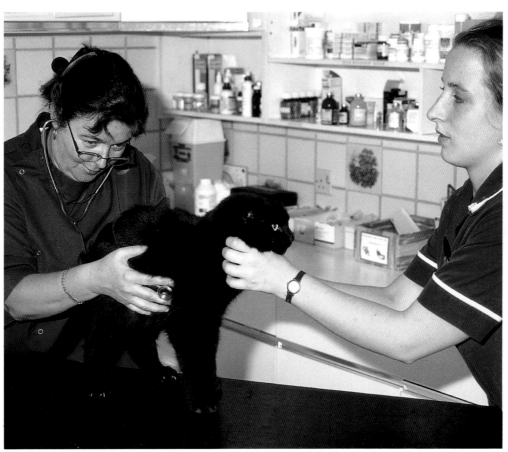

YOUR CAT WON'T THANK YOU FOR THE EXPERIENCE, BUT REGULAR EXAMINATIONS MUST BE ENDURED.

TEMPERATURE-TAKING: A FURTHER (VITAL) INDIGNITY.

If your kitten's mother was immunised, she will have passed on some of her immunity to her foetuses though the placenta while pregnant and, after they were delivered, to her new-borns via the colostrum (the liquid that a nursing mother produces before and after her milk). The concentration of anti-viral antibodies (or maternally-derived antibody, MDA) in colostrum is at its highest for the first day or so after birth,

A MOTHER'S MILK PROVIDES SOME IMMUNITY.

a time when the kitten's bloodstream is also best able to absorb them from its gut. It is therefore important that an entire female's vaccination programme is vigilantly maintained (otherwise a queen may have no immunity to share with her litter) and that a kitten suckles as much as possible during the first days of its life. If you've adopted a feline, and especially a mature female who is either pregnant or has not been spayed, but have no record of any vaccinations that it may have had, take it to the vet's immediately for expert advice.

Because the level of MDA in colostrum is eroded over time, and a kitten's body cannot generate the necessary protective antibodies itself, a kitten should have its first vaccination (nowadays a single injection provides immunity against all three diseases) at the age of around nine weeks. This injection prepares your kitten's immune system to accept a stronger dose, but will not give it adequate protection against the trio of viral cat-killers, which is why your vet will ask you to return it two or three weeks later for a booster. (In the meantime, it is safer not to allow it to go outside in case it comes into contact with any of these serious viruses; because it may also temporarily act as carrier, your vet may advise you to quarantine it from

other felines for a week.) The second dose of vaccine will stimulate your kitten's body to start producing protective antibodies, and thereafter all that your cat will require is an annual booster injection to nudge its body into carrying on the good work.

The first time that your kitten is vaccinated, your vet will give you a record of vaccination, detailing when the first vaccination was given and its brand. Remember to take this record with you when you return your cat for its boosters so that it can be updated (reputable catteries, breeders of pedigree cats and the organisers of cat shows won't accept your feline without it). Try to ensure that you take your cat for its booster at the same time each year – many veterinary surgeries will automatically send you a reminder – because the feline body's maintenance of effective levels of immunity depends on the vaccine being administered just as they are starting to decline. If too long a time has elapsed since your cat's last booster, your vet may advise giving it two boosters two to four weeks apart to kick-start the regeneration of antibodies. If your feline is an indoor cat, don't let yourself be lulled into a false sense of security and be tempted to skip the immunisation programme by believing that,

because it doesn't come into contact with other cats, it won't fall prey to a deadly feline viral disease because you yourself may inadvertently infect it by introducing a virus into your home on your clothes or shoes.

When inspecting your prospective kitten or cat, as well as during the first month or so of its residency in your home while its full immunity has yet to develop, monitor it vigilantly for any symptoms that may indicate that a viral disease has invaded its body. And if you fear the worst, immediately quarantine the feline to reduce the danger of other cats becoming infected and then call your veterinary surgery for instructions. You'll probably be asked to bring your cat in at once for a blood test, but special arrangements will have to be made either to ensure that any other felines in the surgery are segregated from your potentially infected cat or for the vet to visit the patient in your home. The symptoms of feline panleucopenia, feline infectious respiratory disease and feline leukaemia that you should be looking out for (singly, as well as en masse), together with their causes and prognoses, are given below.

Feline panleucopenia

Also known as feline infectious enteritis (FIE) or feline parvovirus, the symptoms of feline panleucopenia are:

- unco-ordination in kittens
- loss of appetite
- chronic thirst, but often an inability to drink
- chronic fatigue and depression
- sitting in a hunched-up position
- pain in the abdomen
- a high temperature
- vomiting frothy matter
- watery and bloody diarrhoea

Cause of infection

Not only can the extremely contagious and long-living feline panleucopenia virus be spread by feline-to-feline contact, but because it is capable of airborne transmission, a cat may be exposed to it if it is brought into the home on your skin, shoes or clothes, via fleas or by sharing an infected cat's bedding, food bowl and litter tray.

Prognosis

Feline panleucopenia is the among the deadliest of all of the incurable viral infections that target cats, and a kitten will be lucky to survive the severe dehydration that it causes.

Although an older cat, particularly if it has been immunised, stands a better chance of coming through feline panleucopenia, infection with this virus will involve a life-or-death struggle and the sick cat will require prolonged nursing (see pages 224 to 226).

Feline infectious respiratory disease

Also known as cat flu, the symptoms of feline infectious respiratory disease are:

- sneezing
- coughing
- catarrh
- laboured or rapid breathing
- pneumonia
- a runny nose
- drooling
- ulcers on the tongue and gums
- weeping eyes, conjunctivitis or the haw pulled over the eye
- loss of appetite
- chronic fatigue
- a high temperature
- vomiting

Cause of infection

The name commonly used to describe feline infectious respiratory disease, cat flu, is somewhat misleading because although the disease's symptoms are similar to those of human influenza, the viral culprits are different, which means that flu-ridden humans can't pass their virus on to cats and vice versa. When a cat contracts feline infectious respiratory disease, it will have been infected by either feline viral rhinotracheitis (FVR) or feline calicivirus, or sometimes both. Infection is caused by close feline-to-feline contact or the inhalation of viral agents when a cat that is already suffering from cat flu sneezes.

Prognosis

Although your cat may have to endure a rough couple of days, and may need a course of antibiotics and devoted nursing to help it pull through, if it survives the onset of cat flu it is likely to live. The virus may, however, remain present in its body, which means that when it is run-down or stressed, mild symptoms of the disease, such as sneezing and a runny nose, may return. In addition, it may become a carrier of cat flu and may therefore infect other cats whose immune systems are not strong enough to resist the disease (so if you have a multi-feline household, ensure that all of your cats are immunised).

The prognosis is more serious for kittens and older cats, however, whose immune systems will be either under-developed on the one hand, or compromised on the other, and who will therefore be unable to put up an effective fight against feline infectious respiratory disease. In such cases, death is a sad probability.

Feline leukaemia

Also known as FeLV (or, erroneously, 'feline AIDS'), the symptoms of feline leukaemia are:

- anaemia (pale gums)
- loss of appetite and weight
- breathing difficulties
- chronic lethargy
- vomiting
- diarrhoea
- skin and mouth infections
- tumours in any part of the body

Cause of infection

Feline leukaemia is most commonly passed from a mother to her kittens, as well as when young cats come into intimate contact (for instance, when bodily fluids are exchanged through fighting, grooming or sexual activity) with infected felines.

Prognosis

Although it is often dubbed 'feline AIDS', feline leukaemia is actually cancer of the blood (which cannot be transmitted to humans). That having been said, however, its effect on the feline immune system is comparable with human AIDS in that a cat may become so weakened that it is incapable of fighting off even a mild infection, not least a serious virus like those detailed previously, making accurate diagnosis difficult. A kitten who contracts the virus will often succumb to it relatively quickly, but if an older cat is infected with feline leukaemia, it may take some time – even years – before the symptoms manifest themselves. Nevertheless, studies have shown that a cat who becomes infected with feline leukaemia is unlikely to survive beyond three years of its initial infection.

Worms and worming

When you take your cat to the vet's for its annual vaccination, it will usually be given a worming pill to prevent its body from becoming host to such common parasites as tapeworms and roundworms or, albeit unusually in Britain, flukes and lung-, heart-, hook-, whip- and threadworms. Although a worm infestation is not life-threatening, if left untreated, it could, over time, sap your feline's vitality and weaken its immune system so that it becomes less resistant to any infections that may threaten its health. Lax hygiene may also result in worms being transferred from a wormy cat to its human carers, which is why you should always wash your hands after handling a cat or cleaning its litter tray (see page 168). An adult cat should be given worming pills specifically targeting round- and tapeworms every four to six months, as your vet advises.

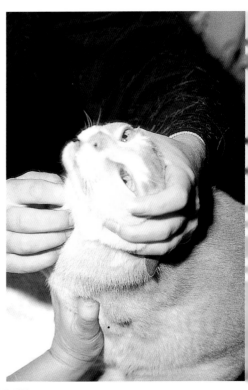

CATS SHOULD BE GIVEN WORMING PILLS AS ADVISED BY YOUR VET.

Apart from crossing from feline to feline, cats can pick up roundworm eggs through eating infested prey. Adult roundworms (*Toxocara* and *Toxascaris*) live in the cat's stomach and small intestine, where they feed off the food that the cat has ingested and breed prolifically, the eggs being passed through the large intestine to emerge in the cat's faeces, traces of which may remain around the anus and be ingested by another cat during a mutual grooming session. Roundworm larvae inhabit cysts within the feline muscular tissue and, more seriously for kittens, sometimes also within the lungs, heart and liver.

Fleas, which are mainly responsible for a tapeworm infestation, swallow tapeworm eggs and then become hosts to their larvae. When a larva-carrying flea in turn sets up home in a cat's fur, the cat may swallow it while grooming, enabling the larva to pass through its digestive system and attach itself to the intestine by means of its hooked scolex, where it will grow into a mature tapeworm, an extremely long, thin parasite, whose body consists of many articulated segments, that lives off the food that the cat is digesting. The individual segments that pass out of the cat's body via the faeces contain the eggs that a flea may ingest, thus perpetuating the pernicious cycle.

CATS MAY INGEST TAPEWORM LARVAE WHILE GROOMING.

147

WASH YOUR HANDS AFTER CLEANING A LITTER TRAY.

When inspecting your kitten or cat for the first time, you should have been looking out for symptoms of worm infestation, which, although they are described on page 97, are worth reiterating in more detail. If a pregnant feline has roundworms (and she should be wormed both before the birth of her kittens and while she is nursing them), her unborn kittens may become infested with their larvae via the placenta, and, following their birth, via her milk, causing both their pre- and post-natal development to be retarded. Along with any unspecific warning signs that a kitten is not in the best of health, look out for a pronounced pot belly and flaky skin, and be especially wary if the kitten is coughing, seems to have been vomiting or has diarrhoea. Further points to note are that if your feline has been sick and

you are very keen-eyed, you may be able discern a mass of wriggling roundworms (which resemble thin threads of fibre) within the vomit. Tapeworm segments, on the other hand, look like grains of rice or melon seeds and may be seen in the fur around a cat's bottom (which may become chronically itchy) or within its faeces.

After you have adopted it, if you think that your kitten or cat may have a worm infestation, note down any relevant symptoms, scoop up a sample of its faeces from the litter tray, place it in a clean, sealable container (remember to wash your hands afterwards) and take it to your veterinary surgery for analysis. If this then shows that your feline does indeed have worms, your vet will prescribe the appropriate course of treatment for your cat.

Fleas and de-fleaing

A FLEA COMB REMOVES SOME, BUT NOT ALL, FLEAS.

from the magnetic attraction that the prospect of a meal of warm feline blood exerts on fleas. Yet with patience, time and the help of dedicated anti-flea measures, a cat that does become a host to fleas can be rid of them. Indeed, with the relatively recent development of effective preventative drops and injections administered by your vet, it need never be troubled by them at all.

Once, on taking our cats to the vet's for their inoculations, we found ourselves sharing the waiting room with a carrier containing a handsome tabby cat, which, the appalled veterinary nurse informed us, had been brought in by its owner with the request that it be put down. The reason given? Flea infestation. Thankfully, there was no question of the vet agreeing to this demand: because the cat was healthy and fleas are banishable, it would instead be rehomed. Its owner's outright rejection of the cat does, however, illustrate the extreme way in which a minority of people react when their cat harbours fleas.

Most cats endure a flea infestation at some point in their lives – it's simply part and parcel of being feline – during a stay in a cattery, even our, predominantly indoor, cats weren't immune

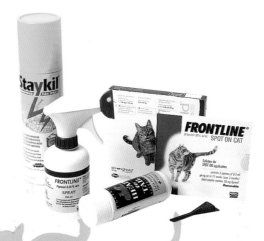

YOU CAN BUY A VARIETY OF ANTI-FLEA PRODUCTS.

Although cat fleas (*Ctenocephalides felis*) are spread by feline-to-feline contact, this needn't be direct because, despite their lack of wings, fleas are famously capable of jumping impressive distances relative to their diminutive size, and their four-stage life cycle enables them

149

to survive for some time without a feline host. Having hopped onto a cat, settled into its fur and started to feed on its blood, after two or three days an adult flea will start laying eggs (two hundred within a flea's lifetime) wherever a cat may be lying – on its bedding or the carpet, for instance – the eggs hatching into larvae a few days later. The developing larvae, which sustain themselves on organic debris, such as flakes of dead skin, evolve into pupae within about two weeks, encasing themselves in cocoons in which they can survive for up to a year before becoming adult. Only then will these parasites need to find a source of fresh blood in order to thrive and perpetuate the flea population's existence.

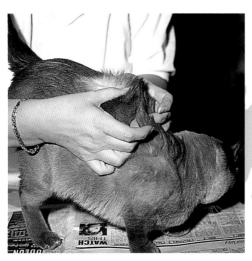

LOOKING FOR FLEAS

Try to pre-empt your cat falling victim to a horde of ravenous fleas by consulting your vet, who will usually recommend a repellent product (which will not harm your feline) that will prevent an infestation should a flea land on it. These are usually regularly administered by means of either an injection or drops that are absorbed through the skin. An alternative is an elasticated collar that has been impregnated with flea-killing chemicals, but the disadvantage of this is both its comparative ineffectiveness, especially in the case of longhairs, and the danger that it may induce an allergy in your cat, resulting in skin irritation and hair loss.

Whether or not you have taken preventative precautions, it's important that you check your cat's fur regularly for signs of an infestation of these pesky parasites, especially during the flea-friendly summer months (although central heating has made them year-round perils). If your cat scratches itself repeatedly and, on investigation, you can see reddish-black specks in its fur, these are likely to be flea droppings, and you will probably also be able to spot the dark-brown fleas responsible scuttling around in its fur. Having confirmed a flea infestation, you will first need to de-flea your cat using a

APPLY FLEA POWDER GENEROUSLY, AND MASSAGE INTO THE SKIN.

proprietary flea powder or spray. Do this by standing your cat on a sheet of newspaper and then applying a generous quantity of the product to the back of its head, making sure that it does not enter its eyes or ears, after which you should gently, but firmly, massage the product into its skin, working from its head to its tail through its flanks, abdomen and chest to its legs and paws. Follow the manufacturer's instructions – you may have to leave the product on the cat for ten minutes or so before brushing it out of the cat's fur and then burning the paper on which the dying fleas have dropped. Thereafter, to prevent reinfestation, you'll have to turn your attention to your home

by washing your cat's bedding, vacuuming each room thoroughly and applying a proprietary environmental anti-flea product to the flooring and furniture. Again, follow the manufacturer's instructions, as it may be that you'll have to repeat the treatment over the next few weeks. Never ignore fleas: not only could your cat develop flea-allergy dermatitis, hair loss or localised infections, but cat fleas have been known temporarily to transfer their attention to humans in desperate circumstances – that is, in the absence of a feline host – and, of course, they can act as intermediate hosts to tapeworm larvae (see page 147).

151

Cat identification

If you give your cat the freedom to roam, there are any number of scenarios that may prevent it from returning home: it may become trapped in a neighbouring garden or shed or fall victim to a road traffic accident, for example, rendering it powerless to find its way back to you. Local newspapers regularly carry reports of cats that have gone missing, or of unidentified house cats that have been found, so if you don't want to suffer the anxiety and heartbreak of your feline friend becoming one of their number and perhaps never being reunited with you, identifying it is a must.

There are two ways of making your cat's identity known: an identity tag attached to its collar or microchipping it. If you decide to opt for the former, make sure that you fit your cat with a collar – perhaps a flea collar – that is designed specially for felines (available from pet shops) and that incorporates an elasticated section so that if your cat catches it on an immovable object there is enough slack to enable it to extract itself without choking. The tag itself (again stocked by pet shops) could either take the form of a hollow, unscrewable metal 'barrel' that contains a strip of paper on which to write your phone number and address or an identity

THE MICROCHIPPING PROCEDURE IS QUICK AND PAINLESS.

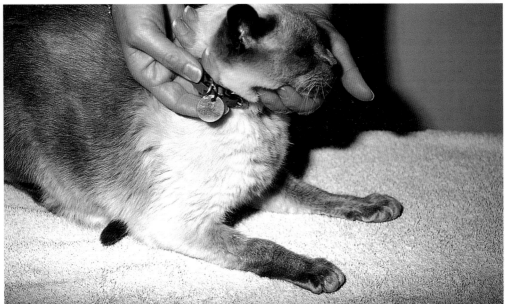

IT'S ADVISABLE TO INCLUDE YOUR PHONE NUMBER AND THE WORD 'REWARD' ON A CAT'S IDENTITY TAG.

disc on which your details can be engraved. (A word of warning if magpies haunt your neighbourhood: Melchior was once gazing out of the window when a magpie, attracted by his glinting identity disc, swooped down out of nowhere and tried to pluck it off through the glass; the traumatised Melchior wouldn't go near that window for weeks!) A tip that may ensure your cat's safe return is simply to specify your phone number and the word 'reward' – greed may tempt even the most feline-indifferent person to contact you. Do not, however, include your cat's name because hearing it uttered could cause it to trust a potential cat-napper.

Many vets now recommend microchipping over a collar and tag. As its name suggests, a microchip is a microscopic chip so small that it can be injected under the loose skin at the back of a cat's neck, where it will remain without causing any discomfort. The microchip contains a code unique to your cat that is registered with a central computer database. Should your cat stray and be brought to a cat-rescue sanctuary, it will be scanned with a dedicated scanner, which will immediately identify the code borne by the microchip and hence, through the database, both your cat and your details, thereby facilitating your feline's return.

NEUTERING REDUCES A FELINE'S URGE TO STRAY.

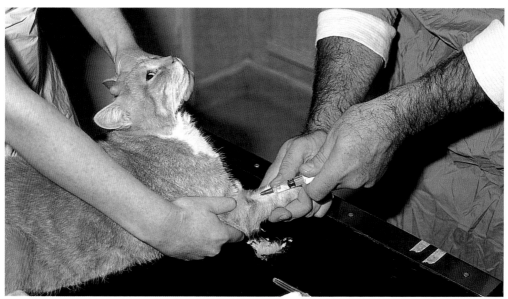

YOUR PRE-OPERATIVE CAT WILL REQUIRE A GENERAL ANAESTHETIC, SO DON'T FEED IT BEFOREHAND.

Neutering your cat

When you were weighing up whether to adopt a male or female cat (see pages 86 to 87), you no doubt decided whether you would have your cat neutered or whether you would be prepared to find homes for any kittens that your female might have or could tolerate a male's roaming and spraying. If you came to the conclusion that you would prefer your kitten or cat not to breed, consult your vet about having your feline neutered when you take it to be immunised. The vet will explain what the operation involves and should also advise you on its optimum timing (if you leave it too long, your kitten may astonish you with the living proof of its sexual maturity).

Vets usually recommend castrating a male cat when it is between four and nine months of age, when it has reached maturity, but any tom-cat habits have not yet become firmly established. Although vets differ as to how soon a female cat should be spayed, the general consensus is between four and six months. (Whatever your cat's sex, your vet will take its individual development into consideration when recommending at what age the operation would best be performed.) Both operations require general anaesthetic, which means that you should not feed or water your cat for at least twelve hours beforehand to prevent it from vomiting while unconscious. A male cat should remain at the surgery for a few hours afterwards – and a female may be kept in overnight – to ensure that it is fully recovered before being allowed to go home.

Castration is a simple procedure in which the testicles are excised (be prepared for your cat's vocal range to become a little higher), while spaying, in which the ovaries and uterus are removed, is a more invasive operation which subsequently requires stitches (and a further trip to the vet's may be required for their removal if they are indissoluble).

When you bring your cat home after the operation, leave it to sleep in peace until it feels more itself, don't give it too much food, try to prevent a female from overexerting herself or worrying at her stitches and keep an eye open for infections. After a few days of rest and recuperation, however, all should be well.

Having kittens

PRIORITISE THE MOTHER-TO-BE'S WELL-BEING DURING THE SIXTY-FIVE DAYS OF HER PREGNANCY.

If, whether by accident or design, you find that your cat is pregnant, her well-being before, during and after the birth of her kittens should become your priority, so as soon as you suspect that she is expecting (and the earliest sign are 'pinked-up', rosy nipples at around three weeks), you should start making preparations for the happy event.

The first thing that you should do is to take the expectant mother to the vet for a thorough check-up to ensure that she is healthy, free from parasites – if not, appropriate treatment will be prescribed – and that no complications are implicated. Following an examination of your cat, your vet will also advise you on the kittens' probable date of birth (around sixty-five days following conception), as well as how to feed and look after their mother in the meantime. Until she goes into labour, there is little active role that you can play in ensuring her welfare beyond adapting her diet to pregnancy so that both she and her unborn kittens remain well nourished. Your vet will probably recommend

A PREGNANT FELINE COULD BE EATING FOR SIX: HERSELF AND FIVE KITTENS.

feeding her more often than usual – she could be eating for five or more – but only towards the end of her term, and ensuring that her diet contains calcium and vitamins A and D (a proprietary cat food formulated specifically for pregnant felines may meet these needs, but consult your vet before making the switch from her usual food).

During the weeks leading up to the birth, your expectant feline will probably spend a considerable amount of time seeking out and investigating suitable spots in which to establish the maternal nest. Her exacting criteria include safety, seclusion, shelter, privacy, warmth and dim light, and if you want to discourage her from setting up camp in a place that would inconvenience the rest of the household, provide her with your preferred alternative. You could, for example, cut away half of one side of a large cardboard box, line the box with layers of newspaper, place it somewhere dark, quiet and draught-free and perhaps half-drape it with an old towel for additional privacy. Encourage her to sit in it, and if she deigns to sleep in it and even starts shredding the newspaper, you'll

157

A CARDBOARD, NEWSPAPER-LINED BIRTHING BED.

know that she's accepted it. If she ignores it, however, and returns to her preferred site, either move the box there shortly before she gives birth or provide an emergency birthing bed, such as newspapers covered with a disposable fabric topped with a clean towel.

When her time approaches, your cat's nipples will start leaking milk and she may continually ask for your reassurance before washing herself intensively and increasingly scratching and squatting as birth becomes imminent. If all goes well, the kittens will emerge one by one, in rapid or slow succession (and it may take up to twelve hours or more before all of the litter have been born). Following each kitten's birth, their

mother will remove its amniotic sac with her tongue, give her new-born a thorough wash, again with her tongue, to stimulate its breathing and encourage its fur to dry, and sever the umbilical cord (in Melchior's case, half of his tail, too) with her teeth. Finally, she will eat the placenta that followed the kitten – behaviour inherited from her wildcat ancestors that both gives the mother additional nutrition and deters predators from locating her and her kittens. It's best to supervise proceedings discreetly, but not to interfere actively unless it's an emergency (ask your vet what danger signs to look out for, and if labour seems to becoming difficult, call him or her out).

With the kittens safely born, the new mother will curl her body around her offspring, both to give them easy access to her milk and to keep them warm. They will remain thus for a day or two, so apart from offering the recumbent mother some water or milk and food, placing a litter tray nearby and checking on the feline family occasionally, you can all take some time off to recover.

NEW FELINE MOTHERS SPEND A CONSIDERABLE AMOUNT OF TIME GROOMING THEIR KITTENS.

Caring for growing kittens

For the first few days of their lives, all that new-born kittens require are the warmth of their mother's body, the nourishment that her milk provides and sleep. Because they are utterly dependent on her, their mother will devote all of her attention to them for the first month or so of their lives, leaving their side only to eat, drink and use the litter tray. She may, however, decide to transfer her litter to a new nest site (thereby obeying an instinct to move them to a place where they will be safer from any danger of a predatory attack), doing this by carrying each kitten in turn by the scruff of its neck. As well as feeding them, she will spend a considerable amount of time keeping them clean, grooming them with her tongue and swallowing their bodily waste, which, for the first four weeks of their lives, they can only produce in response to the stimulus of her tongue licking their bottoms. Unless it is obvious that they are being neglected (unlikely, since most feline mothers lavish exemplary maternal care on their brood), when you may have to call in your vet for advice on remedial action, such as bottle-feeding, it's best to take a hands-off approach. Avoid any active interference, which may upset the mother and jeopardise the kittens' welfare. Do, however, ensure that you provide the

MOST FELINE MOTHERS PROVIDE OUTSTANDING MATERN CARE.

FOR THE FIRST FEW WEEKS OF THEIR LIVES, KITTENS ARE TOTALLY DEPENDENT ON THEIR MOTHER.

mother and, by extension, her kittens, with water and plenty of nutritious food and that you change their bedding regularly. Their mother probably won't mind you handling her kittens gently once their eyes have opened, and, indeed, this is vital if they are to become socialised with humans.

DON'T HANDLE BABIES IF THEIR MOTHER OBJECTS.

Compared with human babies, kittens develop remarkably quickly. Born with their eyes and ears tightly shut and able only to squirm, they initially rely on their senses of smell and touch to locate their mother's teats and latch onto them to feed. Their mother's colostrum gives them some immunity from disease (see page 141), while her milk contains the building blocks of physical development and, if all goes well, they will grow with astonishing speed, doubling their birth weight within a week. While their eyes usually open between four and ten days of age (although it will take a few more weeks before they are able to focus properly), their ears register their mother's communicative purrs, trills and chirrups, they in turn using a

AFTER THEIR EYES HAVE OPENED, HANDLING KITTENS WILL HELP THEM TO BECOME SOCIALISED WITH HUMANS.

range of squeaks to attract her attention. They typically take their first staggering steps at around three weeks of age, after which their mobility improves by leaps and bounds, prompting their harassed mother constantly to call or haul them back to the nest. (When they seem confident that they can control their legs, and are taking responsibility for their own grooming, you could start introducing them to the litter tray.) At around four weeks, when they have mastered control of their limbs, kittens discover the joy of playing games. Playtime may be enormous fun, but it is also a crucial part of the feline learning process, when kittens begin to discover and practise such essential feline life skills as pouncing. Indeed, kittenhood is a

voyage of discovery, supervised closely by their mother, who will try both ensure their safety and to teach them all that they need to know in order to thrive and survive.

By around five weeks of age the litter should be displaying a full set of milk teeth, and the combination of teeth and mobility between three and five weeks, along with their mother's increasing disinclination to feed them at will, signals the time from which some solid food should be introduced to the kittens' diet. Although you should seek your vet's advice on how to supplement and vary their food, you should be safe giving them such highly nutritious dishes (in a shallow bowl) of increasing textural complexity as formula milk for kittens, human baby food, creamed rice, cottage cheese, scraped or minced cooked beef and flakes of steamed fish. They should have been completely weaned off their mother's milk between eight to twelve weeks, after which their diet should consist of a proprietary cat food (see pages 104 to 107) that has been specially formulated for kittens.

KITTENS SHOULD BE WEANED BY THREE MONTHS.

Feeding dos and don'ts

The section on what, and when, to feed your feline in Chapter 2 (see pages 104 to 107) stressed the importance of ensuring that your cat receives the correct balance of the nutrients that are vital to a feline's continued well-being. In practice, all that this usually means for an adult cat is giving it two meals a day of a tinned, foil-packed or dry proprietary food that has been specifically formulated for felines, as well as making sure that a bowl of fresh water is always available. This section delineates some further feeding dos and don'ts.

GIVE YOUR CAT THE OCCASIONAL TREAT.

based on its staple proprietary food. Give it a once or twice-weekly treat of cooked (to ward off toxoplasmosis, see pages 167 to 168), good-quality fish, meat, liver or egg or raw cheese, but don't feed it too much of these foods and certainly not at the expense of its usual proprietary food. If you do, you may expose your feline to dietary deficiencies and may also find yourself pandering to the demands of an ultra-fussy eater.

WATER IS A VITAL ACCOMPANIMENT FOR DRY FOOD.

- Most cats will turn their noses up at food that isn't fresh. Although they usually make an exception for dry proprietary feline food, don't expect them to eat tinned food that has been left over from a previous meal.
- Try to accustom a cat, ideally from kittenhood, to a moderately varied diet, albeit

A SERVING OF TINNED FOOD SHOULD BE FRESH.

- Although liver contains vitamin A, an essential nutrient for felines, overconsumption may cause bone disease, specifically spinal arthritis, so feed it to your cat in moderation. Note that raw liver may result in diarrhoea.
- Your cat may be unable to tolerate milk or cream, either due to an allergy or because lactose (the sugar in cow's milk) does not form part of the natural feline diet. (It by-passes the stomach's digestive juices and is instead consumed by bacteria in the gut, resulting in diarrhoea). If your cat's digestive system reacts badly to it, don't give it milk.

- Don't give your cat raw fish because in its uncooked state the thiaminase enzymes within it break down thiamine, a B vitamin that is vital to feline health. Thiamine deficiency could lead to anaemia or Chastek's paralysis. Don't overcook fish or meat either, because heat also destroys thiamine. A diet that contains a high proportion of fish may lead to skin conditions like eczema or yellow fat disease, so limit your cat's piscine intake.
- Serve your cat cooked food at its preferred temperature — that of warm blood — and not straight from the oven or fridge.
- A large bone to gnaw on will benefit your cat's dental health, but because small or splintered bones could cause a cat to choke, and cooking makes the bones in meat, poultry and fish brittle, always remove such potentially dangerous bones from home-cooked food.
- Cats don't need, or generally greatly enjoy, vegetables, but if you want to interest your feline in some greens, note that cooking them makes them easier for the feline digestive system to process.

MANY CATS HAVE A LACTOSE INTOLERANCE.

- Don't give a healthy cat vitamin or mineral supplements if you're feeding it a proprietary food. Kittens, mothers-to-be, convalescent or old cats may benefit from certain extra vitamins, but be guided by your vet.

- Although health problems may demand that you introduce them, your cat may refuse to countenance any changes to its customary diet. The best way to wean it onto a new food is to introduce it gradually by mixing it with your feline's current foodstuff in increasing proportions. If your cat refuses to eat the food, clear it away, but don't offer what it considers to be a more palatable substitute. When it is hungry enough, it will usually grudgingly consent to eat the novel food that it has previously spurned.

- Don't overfeed your cat or give it constant access to food: a fat feline is susceptible to heart disease and other potentially debilitating conditions.

- If your cat has been ill or is old, it may have lost its appetite and its sense of smell may have been dulled. When trying to entice a convalescent or old cat to eat in order to build up its strength, tempt it with small amounts of strongly smelling food, such as tinned tuna, pilchards or sardines or choice morsels of fresh meat.

- When a cat reaches a venerable age, it's better to give it three or four small meals of its favourite foods a day instead of the two that it enjoyed in its prime. This strategy is more friendly to an ageing digestive system.

IF YOUR CAT ENJOYS A WELL-BALANCED DIET, IT WILL BE LESS LIKELY TO STEAL YOUR SUPPER.

Feline-related hygiene measures

FELINES ARE SCRUPULOUS SELF-GROOMERS . . .

Although ill or old cats, who may find self-grooming or reaching their litter tray difficult, may need a helping human hand, most adult cats are rigorous about maintaining high standards of feline hygiene, grooming themselves both thoroughly and regularly, as well as scrupulously covering their faeces with either earth or cat litter. (Melchior is untypically laissez-faire about the latter, instead leaving the tedious business of covering-up to the more fastidious Caspar.) There still remain certain risks of infection that are out of a feline's control, however, which it's important to take steps to address in the interests of maintaining both your cat and your family's health. The most basic are keeping your cat's bedding and bowls clean, as well as regularly checking its body carefully for signs of any physical problems. Others include the prevention and, if necessary, control of worms and fleas (see pages 146 to 151) and yet more the treatment of any infectious skin conditions – fungal dermatitis like ringworm, for example (see page 198) – that your cat may develop and then pass on to you or your family.

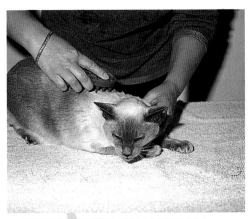

. . . BUT MOST REQUIRE A LITTLE HUMAN HELP.

Counted among the few other conditions, known as zoonoses, that can be transmitted from felines to humans is cat-scratch fever (whose cause is exactly as its name suggests), which can result in a mild temperature and inflammation of the lymph nodes in humans, so always wash and disinfect any wound inflicted by a cross cat. A more serious zoonosis is

COMBAT TOXOPLASMOSIS WITH RUBBER GLOVES.

toxoplasmosis, a flu-like disease caused by the protozoan parasite *Toxoplasma gondii*, which your cat may become host to through eating infected raw meat (because heat destroys the parasites, it's advisable to cook any meat that you give it), excreting the parasites in its faeces. If a pregnant woman contracts toxoplasmosis, serious implications may ensue for her unborn child, ranging from malformation of the skull and blindness to liver infections and even stillbirth, so mothers-to-be should ensure that their skin never comes into contact with feline faeces. In fact, the following advice applies to all cat-owners.

- When cleaning a litter tray, always wear disposable plastic gloves, throw them away after use and wash your hands.

- Remove faeces from the litter tray as soon as possible, using a litter scoop, which you should store in a plastic bag.

- Thoroughly clean and disinfect the litter tray at least once a week, using hot water and disinfectant (but check the label to make sure that the disinfectant is cat-friendly because some can poison cats).

- At the same time, replace the cat litter (this should be done at least once a week, although a top-up will usually suffice after using the litter scoop).

- Wear gloves when gardening because it is a rare garden that does not harbour feline faeces.

Because children are especially vulnerable to attack by zoonoses, ensure that they never handle feline faeces (be wary about letting them play in sandpits which are left uncovered when not in use) and encourage them to wash their hands after handling or grooming a cat.

Although this isn't always practical, hand-washing is a sensible precaution for adults, too, and a vital one before food is prepared. Similarly, discourage your cat from jumping onto kitchen surfaces, but, if it does so, disinfect them immediately.

Grooming your cat

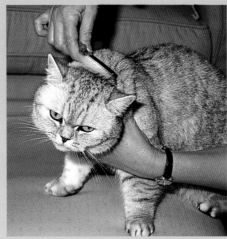

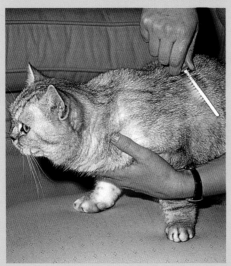

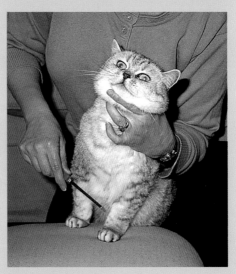

IF YOU DO LITTLE ELSE IN THE WAY OF GROOMING, AT LEAST COMB YOUR CAT USING A COMB APPROPRIATE FOR ITS COAT. A SHORTHAIRED FELINE SHOULD BE COMBED ONCE A WEEK, WHILE A LONGHAIRED CAT MAY NEED DAILY GROOMING. STARTING FROM ITS HEAD, WORK ALONG ITS BACK TO ITS TAIL BEFORE TURNING YOUR ATTENTION TO ITS UNDERSIDE.

Your cat will spend a considerable amount of time grooming its fur, and will make an admirable job of it, too. A longhaired cat, however, will usually not be able to keep on top of the task unaided, and a shorthair will also need a helping hand to keep its coat in peak condition. (If you are planning to show your cat, immaculate grooming is essential, but because pre-show grooming is an art form and this section deals with grooming basics, consult a specialist authority or publication for further guidance.) An indoor cat's claws will furthermore require regular clipping, and whether or not your cat is an indoor or outdoor feline, your vet may advise you to institute a tooth-cleaning regime. (See pages 113 to 117 for details on grooming equipment.)

All of these tasks are easily mastered, but if you are unsure how best to perform them, seek your vet's advice. And in the unlikely event that you really aren't equal to grooming your cat, a regular trip to a local feline beauty salon is an alternative option. Never, however, succumb to the temptation to have your cat declawed: not only does minimal attention render such drastic action unnecessary, but the removal of an essential part of a cat's self-defensive and climbing equipment is unkind, to put it mildly.

Because most domestic cats moult all year round, dead hairs accumulate on their coat which they will ingest while grooming, the resultant build-up being vomited up as sausage-shaped furballs. Not only will regular combing (once a week for shorthairs and daily for longhairs) minimise this uncomfortable problem, but it also provides an opportunity for you to keep an eye open for any skin problems or parasites, as well as increasing the bond between you and your feline. Their sheer abundance of fur makes it especially difficult for longhairs to prevent the build-up of tangles which, if not dealt with immediately, could result in such severe matting that the only solution is either to cut out the clump with a pair of round-tipped scissors or, in extreme instances, for the vet to shave your sedated cat. The sooner you accustomise your cat to being groomed, the easier the process will subsequently become. Your cat's acquiescence can also be encouraged by holding the back of its neck firmly as you comb from its head along its back and tail before turning it over to address its underside. I comb our cats, using the appropriate steel comb for their different coat types, immediately before feeding them, a cunning endure-and-reward strategy that I've found very effective. Although it isn't always

MOST SHORTHAIRED CATS MAKE AN ADMIRABLE JOB OF KEEPING THEIR COATS SPICK-AND-SPAN.

GROOMING TIME GIVES YOU THE CHANCE TO CHECK YOUR CAT'S COAT FOR FLEAS AND SKIN PROBLEMS.

cat care-fundamentals

essential after a thorough combing, many feline coats benefit from having any loose hairs removed through being brushed with a natural- or nylon-bristled brush for the body, a toothbrush for the facial fur and finally perhaps a slicker brush to impart some sheen.

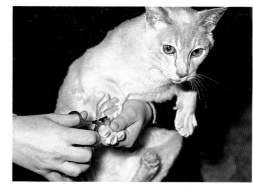

SQUEEZE THE BASE OF EACH CLAW IN TURN.

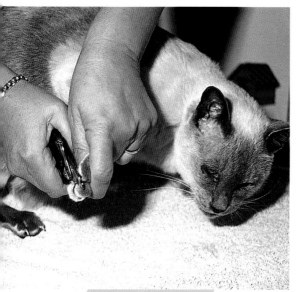

CLAW-CLIPPING IS A MUST FOR INDOOR CATS.

IF YOU WANT TO AVOID BEING BITTEN . . .

An indoor cat may object to having its claws clipped, in which case prevent any outraged struggling by swaddling it in a blanket or towel so that only its head and front paws are protruding from the bundle. Squeeze the base of each claw in turn with one hand to extend it and then trim it with clippers wielded by your

. . . USE A BRUSH TO CLEAN A CAT'S TEETH.

other hand. Because it contains blood vessels, it's important not to cut into the living quick (you'll see it as a pale-pink triangle), so only trim the translucent tips. You'll probably need to do this every two to four weeks, and the occasion will also provide a convenient chance to check that the paw pads haven't sustained any wounds or thorns.

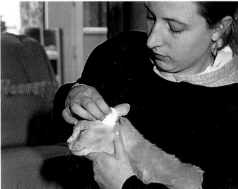

CLEAN A CAT'S EARS WITH DAMP COTTON WOOL.

TRIM ONLY THE CLAWS' TRANSLUCENT TIPS.

Finally, grooming time presents an opportunity to check the condition of your cat's eyes and ears; if they look a little gungy, clean them gently with some cotton wool moistened with tepid water. If any changes in its ears, eyes, teeth, claws or skin give you cause for concern, take your cat to the vet because they may indicate a potentially serious health problem.

If it's considered necessary, your vet will advise you how often to clean your cat's teeth, a technique that is easily learned (ask for a demonstration), although you must never apply too much pressure. At the same time, check that your cat's gums are rosy pink – an indication of good health – and that there isn't a build-up of tartar on the teeth themselves, which would require scaling by your vet.

BE VERY GENTLE WHEN WIPING A CAT'S EYES.

Fostering feline fitness

FEEL YOUR CAT'S BODY TO CHECK FOR WEIGHT GAIN.

Fat feral felines are almost unheard of, for not only is food harder to come by for ferals than for house cats, but they have to expend considerable time and energy in procuring it, and their predatory exercise regime keeps them fit and lean. Domestic cats, by contrast, often need only to miaow persistently for a meal to materialise, the only parts of their bodies that they exert in their quest for food being their vocal cords. And if a domestic cat is also an indoor cat, which has limited opportunities for regular physical activity, it will be in greater danger of putting on weight and losing muscle tone. Although cats are rarely inclined to eat for greed's sake, for a bored indoor feline, the highlight of the day is the materialisation of a full feeding bowl rather than the thrill of the chase, and it may thus pile on the pounds. Excessive weight gain, which puts extra strain on every organ, especially the heart, is just as much a danger to feline as to human health, so it is vital not to collude in creating a fat cat. When grooming your cat, take the time to feel its ribs, and if they are difficult to distinguish because they are padded with fat, consult your vet about instituting a weight-loss programme (and many proprietary cat-food ranges now include slimming diets).

YOUR VET MAY ADVISE WEIGHING YOUR CAT REGULARLY.

Because weight gain creeps upwards when more calories are ingested than expended, the best way in which to prevent your cat from becoming fat is to ensure that it has ample opportunity for exercise. Access to the great outdoors is usually enough, but if your cat is confined to a small garden, consider building an outdoor run or activity centre, for example, including branches arranged at different heights for your cat to scale. If your cat is an indoor cat and your home is limited in size, two solutions to the exercise conundrum are to construct an indoor climbing frame or to devote at least half an hour a day to playing with your feline. Not only will a vigorous game enable your cat to exercise its muscles, it will also provide mental stimulation and strengthen the bond between the human and feline playmates. Be they indoor or outdoor felines, kittens or adults, all cats

hanker after playtime, so even if you aren''t around to participate, provide your cat with lots of toys with which to entertain itself.

SOME CATS DEVISE THEIR OWN KEEP-FIT REGIMES.

GARDEN PATROLS WILL KEEP AN OUTDOOR CAT TRIM.

PLAYTIME GIVES THE FELINE BODY A WORK-OUT.

175

KITTENS ARE FAMOUSLY FOCUSED ON PLAY, AN ACTIVITY THAT NOT ONLY HELPS THEM TO LEARN AND HONE THEIR HUNTING SKILLS, BUT ALSO STRENGTHENS THEIR MUSCLES AND SHARPENS THEIR REFLEXES. THE BODIES OF OLDER CATS, TOO, WILL BENEFIT FROM THE EXERCISE THAT PLAYTIME INVOLVES, ESPECIALLY IF THEY ARE INDOOR FELINES.

Opinion is divided about walking cats as we do dogs. Those that are against the practice point out that a cat's heart and lungs cannot comfortably sustain prolonged periods of exercise (see page 36) and that going on long, companionable rambles is furthermore alien to the feline nature – a cat is not, after all, a pack animal, but an individualistic creature focused on its core territory – and what happens when the pair of you encounter a dog? Advocates of cat-walking, by contrast, counter that many cats (especially Oriental breeds like Siamese) enjoy walking with their owners and assert that the exercise is good for them. If you decide to try walking your cat, make sure that you fit it with an elasticated harness designed specifically for cats, never attach a lead to its collar or drag it after you and only stroll à deux for short distances. You never know, after a few weeks of accustomisation to this alien practice, your cat may take to being promenaded (unlike ours, who sat down mutinously and refused to budge, all the while wailing piteously). Ultimately, however, the decision as to whether or not it's amenable to 'walkies' will be made by your cat, not you.

MOST CATS PREFER TO WALK ALONE.

Training your cat

IS IT TIME TO BUY YOUR CAT A SCRATCHING POST?

Unlike dogs, cats are notoriously resistant to being trained – if anything, it's they who train their human housemates. Nevertheless, if you take the word 'train' to mean accustomising a cat to certain behavioural patterns rather than teaching it tricks, then it is possible to train it. In many instances, your cat won't need much training anyway: once an indoor cat has made its litter tray's acquaintance, for example, it will typically become instantly house-trained (see page 109). Because feline laws and imperatives differ from those of humans, however, your cat may not, for instance, understand why scratching at furniture is forbidden when it's praised for stropping vigorously at its scratching post or why it's shouted at for jumping onto a kitchen surface to grab a tasty morsel when you

MAKE CLEAR THAT HUMAN FOOD IS NOT FOR CATS.

BAN YOUR CAT FROM KITCHEN SURFACES.

otherwise willingly provide it with food. If your reaction is ambiguous or inconsistent, it will thus become confused about what is acceptable behaviour and what isn't. Remember, too, that there may be a reason for your cat's 'bad' behaviour: felines need to keep their claws in trim, for example, so if it is scratching the furniture, is this because it can't do so on a tree and you haven't provided a scratching post?

There are certain house rules that you'll have to drum into your cat if you are to live together healthily and harmoniously, and this is most

A FELINE WILL SOON LEARN TO USE ITS CAT FLAP.

TAKE A CONSISTANT LINE ON WINDOWSILLS.

179

TRAIN YOUR CAT TO STEER CLEAR OF DANGER AREAS.

TRYING TO TRAIN YOUR CAT USING TERROR TACTICS CAN BE COUNTERPRODUCTIVE.

successfully done by using the twin approaches of clarity and consistency. Before welcoming a feline into your home, decide what sort of habits you will tolerate and what is absolutely forbidden. Even if a cat continues to think in its heart of hearts that your rules are illogical, if you stick firmly to them and it knows that you will be displeased with it every time that it breaks them, it will reluctantly learn to comply.

DECIDE ON A FURNITURE RULE AND THEN STICK TO IT.

When training a cat, there are two strategies that you could follow: aversion therapy and rewarding correct behaviour. Aversion therapy is best employed in emergency situations when a cat threatens to do something that could endanger its safety, for example, leaping onto a hot cooking hob, the response to which should be active discouragement. Conveying your disapproval with a loud and stern 'No!' will usually suffice if repeated each time that your cat misbehaves. Another way of training a cat to desist from doing something that irks you is

TRAINING CAN PLAY A CRUCIAL ROLE IN SAFEGUARDING YOUR CAT'S PHYSICAL WELFARE.

to squirt a pump-action plant spray filled with water in its direction; although the mist of water droplets will not harm the cat, it can have spectacularly successful results if used in judicious moderation. And if a particular spot repeatedly receives a cat's unwanted attentions, try dabbing some vinegar or lemon juice onto it, the smell of which is so repellent to a feline that it will keep its distance. Never, however, hit a cat because this will simply cause it to distrust and fear you, often resulting in even more unco-operative behaviour because it has linked the punishment with you rather than the feline action that preceded it.

Discouraging bad behaviour is one thing, but training your cat to do something that wouldn't naturally occur to it, or that it would definitely prefer not to do – like returning home at night when it would rather be out hunting – is quite another. I suspect that the question that a cat asks itself when a human makes an incomprehensible demand of it is 'Why? What's in it for me?' to which the best answer is 'food' (think about how rapidly your cat responds to the sound of its meals being prepared and how affectionately it treats you immediately before you place its food bowl in front of its nose). It may take repeated attempts, but if you reward your feline with its favourite titbit each time that it complies with your wishes, it will soon learn the lesson of human-prompted cause and feline-satisfying effect.

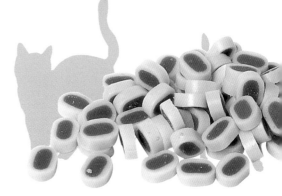

REWARD GOOD BEHAVIOUR WITH A TASTY TREAT.

When the human's away . . .

When planning a stay away from home, making provision for your cat should be high on your list of things to do.

If it's only for a night, put out enough food and water to cover evening and morning meals, make sure that the litter tray is fit for feline use and, if you have an outdoor cat, confine it to your home until your return. Longer human absences require more careful planning, however, because you cannot leave your cat – who, after all, depends on you for food, water, shelter and company – to fend for itself alone.

ENSURE THAT YOUR CAT WILL BE WELL CARED FOR IF YOU HAVE TO LEAVE IT HOME ALONE.

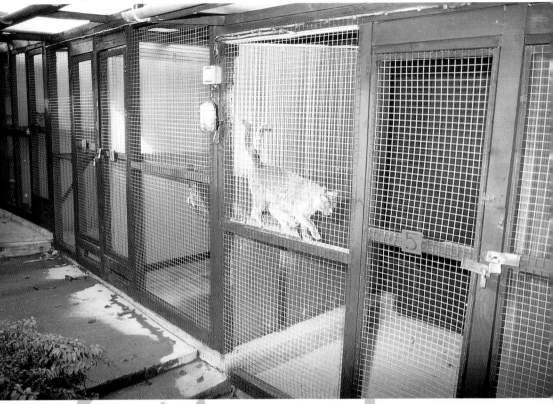

A GOOD CATTERY SHOULD PROVIDE YOUR CAT WITH ITS OWN RUN SO THAT IT CAN TAKE SOME EXERCISE.

The kindest solution, the feline identity being focused on its home territory, is to stock up with sufficient food and cat litter to cover your period of absence and to arrange for a neighbour or cat-sitter to come into your home twice a day (or even better, to move in) to provide your cat with food, water and a bit of affection, to clean its litter tray and to make sure that it remains in good health (remember to leave your vet's details and to show its temporary carer where its carrier is kept in case of emergencies). If you have a cat flap, an outdoor cat could still enjoy trips outside, but for security's sake you may prefer it to become an indoor cat while you're away (don't forget to shut all of the windows). Alternatively, you could take your feline, along with its cat-care accoutrements, to stay with a friend or relative.

The only other option – and an expensive one – is to board your cat at a cattery, where it will be provided with food (although you may be asked to provide its usual fare if it is a fussy eater or has special dietary requirements) and shelter. Before booking your cat into a cattery (ask your vet to recommend one), try to inspect it to check that the premises appear clean and well-run and that your cat will have its own, relatively spacious, run, where it will be warm and dry and will have no contact with other feline boarders to by-pass the twin dangers of fights and infection. Along with your cat, remember to take its vaccination record and perhaps a favourite object or piece of bedding to act as a comfort-blanket.

USE A CARRY CAGE TO INTRODUCE YOUR CAT TO IT'S TEMPORARY HOME IN THE CATTERY.

Felines on the move

MANY CATS ACTIVELY RESIST BEING BUNDLED INTO THEIR CARRIERS, AND YOU MAY HAVE TO RESTRAIN YOURS FIRST.

Whether you are taking your cat to the vet's, to stay at a cattery or to your new house, you will need to confine it to a cat-carrier (see pages 99 to 100) for the duration of the trip. Before doing so, you will, of course, have to catch your cat, which can be quite a palaver if, like our two, it tends to flee as soon as it catches sight of its carrier. We have learned that the most effective way of transferring our cats to their carriers is first to shut any doors leading outside before extracting the carriers from their storage place. Then we calmly herd our reluctant felines into one room, closing the door before ushering each cat into its respective carrier. Their response to being 'caged' is a steady stream of anxious howls, which they keep up for a while in the car, although on longer trips they eventually settle down and snooze fitfully. If your cat faces a really long trip, it may be advisable not to give it food or water for a few hours beforehand if you can't ensure that it will be able to use a litter tray (within a stationary vehicle with the doors and windows closed) en route. If you're taking your cat abroad, remember that it will need to be microchipped (see page 153) and to travel with its own pet passport (provided by your vet), and if it will be a flying feline, check ahead with both the airline and country of destination to see what arrangements you'll need to make.

SWADDLING A CAT IN A TOWEL WILL NEUTRALISE ITS CLAWS, MAKING IT EASIER TO PLACE IT IN THE CARRIER.

CONFINING A CAT TO ITS CARRIER FOR THE DURATION OF MOVING DAY WILL ENSURE ITS SAFETY.

When moving house, you'll have to take steps to ensure that your cat doesn't become unsettled by the drastic changes occurring within its home environment and doesn't go missing as a result. Before the upheavals start on moving day, confine your cat to one room, along with its water bowl and litter tray, and warn any removal personnel not to enter that room; if this isn't possible, a less comfortable alternative is to confine it to its carrier. When it's time to leave your old home, never load your cat onto a removal van, but instead let it travel with you in its carrier so that it can derive some reassurance from your presence. Make sure that your feline's food, bowls, litter tray and litter are easily accessible – ideally stow them in the boot of your car – and haven't been packed away in an unmarked box. Once you've arrived at your new abode, again either keep your cat confined to its carrier or release it into a room where it'll be undisturbed and shut the door. After your possessions have been unloaded and relative peace prevails, introduce your feline to its new home by taking the same measures that you used when you welcomed it into your previous house (see pages 128 to 129) and don't allow it to go outside for a week or so until you are sure that it views its new abode as home.

DON'T LET YOUR CAT INSPECT ITS NEW HOME UNTIL THE WORST OF THE UPHEAVALS ARE OVER.

189

Caring for an older cat

Although our cats are now twelve years old, they haven't fundamentally changed since they officially became adult felines at nine months. That having been said, they have become rather more *blasé* about the joys of active playtime and, being semi-indoor cats, have a tendency to put on weight, which is why their vet has advised feeding them a proprietary cat food formulated for senior felines who need to slim.

How can you tell that your cat is entering old age? Working out the human equivalent of a feline's age is an imprecise science, and there is some argument about the traditional assertion that multiplying the years that your cat has lived by seven is a good general rule of thumb. Most authorities, however, agree that after notching up twelve years a cat is in its mid-sixties, after fifteen years its mid-seventies, while after twenty years it's approaching its centenary. Just as in

AS A CAT AGES, IT STARTS TO SLOW DOWN AND SPENDS MORE TIME SLEEPING.

KITTENS AND OLDER CATS HAVE VERY DIFFERENT DIETARY REQUIREMENTS.

humans, a feline's ageing process varies according to the individual, so it's best to monitor your cat for signs that its age may be catching up with it. These include loss of appetite, weight and condition (possibly indicating degeneration of the liver or kidney disease), increased thirst, constipation or incontinence, stiffness, skin tumours and dental problems (see Chapter 4 for further details). If you have any cause for concern, take your cat to the vet, who will advise the appropriate remedial treatment, which will often involve a dietary adjustment.

Because older cats have an increased requirement for vitamins and minerals, your vet may advise switching it to a diet specifically formulated to meet this need at a relatively early age (ours were eight, or approaching fifty human years). When it has become clear that your cat has graduated to the ranks of the really senior citizens of the feline world, your vet may

191

advocate feeding it four small meals a day, as well as a diet that contains dietary fibre to counter constipation and is rich in protein and fat to provide its body with extra energy and insulation. An older cat will spend most of its time sleeping, but when it awakes its first thought will typically be 'I'm awake: I must be hungry!' and because food may be one of its few remaining pleasures, oblige it with a small, but highly palatable, meal. Make sure that it

has a cosy bed in a warm spot in which to sleep and that its food and water bowls, as well as its litter tray, are close by. It will also increasingly appreciate your company and affection, so take the time to stroke and talk to it and keep up a gentle grooming regime (an older cat's increasing lack of mobility makes self-grooming difficult). If your cat begins to suffer from failing eyesight and hearing, make sure that you don't disorientate it by moving familiar objects around

A FELINE SENIOR CITIZEN'S WORLD REVOLVES AROUND THE TWIN PLEASURES OF SLEEP AND FOOD.

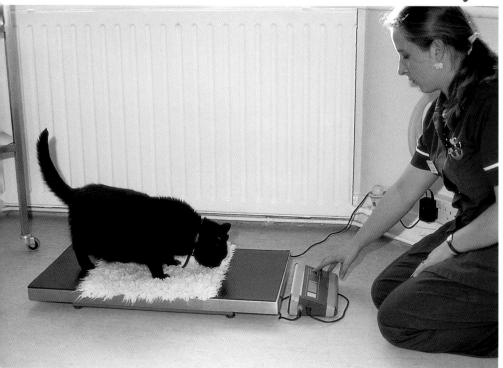

OLD CATS TEND TO SUFFER FROM WEIGHT LOSS, AND YOUR VET MAY ADVISE REGULAR WEIGHING SESSIONS.

and note that these senses won't warn it of the approach of potential dangers.

When caring for an older cat, the golden rule is to be guided by your vet, who should see it every three months or so, or as recommended, to monitor its health. Your vet will be able to ascertain with clinical accuracy when your cat is reaching the end of its natural days or when the pain caused by a chronic condition can no longer be alleviated and your cat's quality of life has plummeted irrevocably. If euthanasia is recommended, accept that your experienced vet, who has its best interests at heart, is certain that there is no hope that your cat will recover and recognises that prolonging its life will condemn it to further suffering. Remember, too, that the euphemism that is frequently used for euthanasia, 'putting to sleep', accurately describes the administering of a painless injection that is the last act of kindness that you can authorise for your old friend.

193

4

Feline afflictions and their treatment

 feline afflictions

In this chapter, we'll take a voyage around the feline body to home in on the afflictions to which a cat's skin and coat, ears, eyes, nose and mouth may fall prey. Certain ailments are minor, while others may be symptomatic of more serious threats to a cat's health, some of which are detailed in Chapter 5. No matter how trivial they may seem, as soon as you notice that your feline is suffering from any of these symptoms, it's important to take the appropriate measures to restore it to full physical fitness, the first usually being taking it to be examined by your vet, who will instruct you how best to care for it. Because you may be advised to monitor its vital signs, to administer pills and other forms of medication or to nurse your under-par cat, basic guidance on how to perform these procedures is also given in this chapter. As ever, however, when identifying and treating feline ailments, be guided by your vet.

YOUR CAT MAY FALL VICTIM TO ANY NUMBER OF FELINE AFFLICTIONS.

Afflictions of the skin and coat

Two of the most common afflictions of the skin and coat that affect cats – flea infestation (see pages 149 to 151) and matted fur due to inefficient grooming (see pages 169 to 170), as well as the necessary remedial actions – were detailed in Chapter 3. In addition, keep a hawk-like eye open for all of the following afflictions of the skin and coat during your regular grooming sessions. Although you can easily treat some yourself, others will require the specialist advice of your vet, as well as prescription medication.

Symptoms

- Round patches of bald skin, maybe crusty around the edges: see ringworm.
- Red or purple bean-like protrusions: see ticks.
- Grey insects and tiny white eggs: see lice.
- Flaky and bald patches, inflammation and chronic itchiness: see mange mites.
- Minute yellow spots: see harvest mites.
- Tiny yellow larvae within an open wound: see maggots.
- Thinning hair on the abdomen and lower back: see alopecia.
- Chronic itchiness, scabs, weeping lesions or localised loss of hair, particularly on the legs and back: see dermatitis and eczema.
- Greasy fur, crusty skin and hair loss around the tail: see stud tail.
- Greasy fur and spots on the chin or lips: see feline acne.

Ringworm

Despite its misleading name, ringworm is not a type of worm, but a form of fungal dermatitis (*Microsporum canis*) that is transmitted by direct contact with infected animals or even inanimate objects and that manifests itself as round patches of bald skin, sometimes crusty around the periphery, usually on the head, ears and forepaws. Among the most infectious of all of the zoonoses, ringworm is easily transmitted to humans, especially children and women, and speed is of the essence in banishing it. If you suspect that your cat has ringworm, whisk it to the vet, who will inspect the lesions under ultra-violet light. If they appear fluorescent, and ringworm is therefore confirmed, you will be given a course of anti-fungal tablets and ointment or shampoo with which to treat your cat. Remember to wash your hands after administering any medication, to burn infected bedding and thereafter to keep your cat's immediate environment scrupulously clean. You may also be advised to quarantine your cat until it is ringworm-free, which may take many weeks.

Ticks

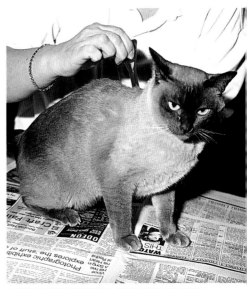

ONLY A DEAD TICK WILL RELINQUISH ITS GRIP.

Ticks are small, eight-legged parasites that lurk in grassy and woodland habitats waiting for a warm-blooded host onto which to latch with their mouthparts. Your cat may pick up sheep or deer ticks (*Ixodes ricinus*) or hedgehog ticks (*Ixodes hexagonus*) either while out on patrol or by coming into contact with an infested animal, and you will see them as red or purple bean-like protrusions on the skin. Because there is a danger that a tick bite may impart a number of potentially debilitating diseases, notably Lyme disease – to you, as well as your cat – and cause localised infections, you must rid it of these parasites immediately. They cannot simply be pulled off, however, for once they have sunk their mouthparts into their host's skin, ticks excrete a substance that cements them firmly into place, so that although you may have removed their bodies, their mouthparts will remain embedded within the skin, redoubling the risk of infection. To force a tick to relinquish its grip, you therefore have to kill the tick while it is still attached to your cat, which can be done by applying a suffocating layer of petroleum jelly, nail-varnish remover, surgical spirit or alcohol with a cotton bud and leaving it to do its work before removing the dead tick with a pair of tweezers. Alternatively, you could treat a tick-infested cat with a proprietary spray (stocked by most veterinary surgeries).

Lice

Tiny grey parasites, lice (*Felicola*) are spread through contact with infested felines or objects, but are usually only suffered by cats in poor general condition. One type of cat louse sucks a cat's blood, while its biting fellow feeds on dead skin and fur. The first sign of an infestation is when a cat starts scratching itself repeatedly, whereupon you may be able to discern the culprit insects or their minute white eggs (nits) on its skin. If left to thrive, lice can cause a cat

to become dangerously anaemic and sickly, so bathe an infested cat with an insecticidal shampoo, apply a follow-up preparation and use a fine-toothed comb to rid its coat of both the lice and their nits, a process that will probably have to be repeated.

REMOVE LICE AND NITS WITH A FINE-TOOTHED COMB.

Mange mites

The mange mite that occasionally targets cats is *Notoedres cati*, which, because it embeds itself deep within the feline skin, causes the surrounding area to become severely irritated and inflamed and may also result in hair loss. Evidence of excruciatingly itchy mange-mite infestation is typically seen on the ears and head, in the form of patches of flaky and bald

199

skin. Spread by feline-to-feline contact, mange is uncommon in house cats that are well cared for, but, if it occurs, your vet will advocate treatment with antibiotics and insecticides.

Harvest mites

SCRATCHING IS A SIGN OF CHIGGER INFESTATION.

As their name suggests, the heyday of harvest mites, or chiggers (*Trombicula autumnale*), is during the late summer, when these parasites may make the leap from grass to cat. The signs of a harvest-mite infestation are the tiny yellow spots that pinpoint where the parasites have burrowed under the feline skin, causing the cat to scratch the irritated areas. The infestation is

relatively short-lived, however, particularly if treated with a preparation recommended by your vet.

Maggots

It is usually only neglected felines and cats in extremely poor condition that succumb to maggots, the larvae that hatch from the eggs of flies that have alighted upon matted fur, an open wound or chronically inflamed skin, often around the rectum if a cat is suffering from persistent diarrhoea, and especially during the summer. Notwithstanding the cat's pre-existing poor health, which will have prevented it from swatting away the culprit flies in the first place, an infestation of maggots is deadly serious because these parasites will literally eat away and poison its flesh. It is vital that the cat sees the vet as soon as possible, but initial first-aid can be administered by cutting away clumps of dirty fur, removing any visible yellow maggots with tweezers and wiping the affected areas with a feline-friendly antiseptic solution.

Alopecia

Neutered cats are prone to the form of hair loss called alopecia, which is caused by hormonal imbalances and causes the fur on the abdomen and lower back to thin significantly, albeit without causing any irritation. Because there is no danger of infection, and the cat is suffering no discomfort, there is nothing that you need do, although your vet may recommend a dietary adjustment or hormone-therapy treatment (HRT).

Dermatitis and eczema

SKIN ALLERGIES PROVOKE CHRONIC ITCHING.

You will first be alerted to the presence of the allergic conditions dermatitis and eczema in your cat if it constantly scratches and licks itself – particularly its limbs and back – because these skin conditions cause chronic itching. Although not in themselves serious, the cat may lick the affected areas so frantically in its attempt to alleviate the maddening itchiness that either scaliness, scabs or weeping lesions, and hence infections, may develop, along with hair loss. Having first checked that no parasites, especially fleas, are responsible (and if they are, take the appropriate countermeasures), present your cat to the vet. It may be that it has a dietary or environmental allergy or else a hormonal imbalance, which the vet will help you to identify and treat. Whatever the cause, cleaning and drying the skin prior to the regular application of a soothing preparation will probably be prescribed, sometimes along with the wearing of an Elizabethan collar (see page 222) to prevent your cat from further aggravating its skin condition.

Stud tail

Despite its macho name, stud tail can sometimes occur in entire females and neutered males, as well as in strutting toms. Tom cats are, however, more prone to this testosterone-

influenced skin condition, in which the oil-producing glands at the base of the tail become blocked and the fur becomes covered in grease, sometimes causing hair loss and encrustation of the skin. Although the only danger to health inherent in stud tail is if the skin becomes inflamed (when antibiotics will be required), you may wish to clean the area with a mild shampoo.

Feline acne

Teenagers may be comforted to know that cats can get blackheads and spots, too, and for the same reasons as humans: the clogging-up of the skin's sebaceous glands, to which a build-up of grease from food residues may contribute. Feline acne typically erupts on the lips and chin, areas which a cat finds difficult to reach while grooming. Although this skin condition usually clears up on its own, you should monitor any outbreaks of feline acne for the development of abscesses (see page 237), which could have serious consequences. If a spot looks particularly angry, you could encourage it to burst by dabbing it with cotton wool soaked in warm water and then apply a feline-friendly antiseptic. If your cat suffers from chronic acne, however, consult your vet, who may prescribe a course of antibiotics.

Afflictions of the ears

APPLYING EAR DROPS REQUIRES CAUTION.

You will usually be alerted to any trouble brewing within your cat's ears if you see it scratching them repeatedly or shaking its head – signs of chronic irritation – whereupon you should immediately take a closer look. As well

terms of infection or damage to the ear's delicate internal structure could be serious. Similarly, if ear drops are prescribed, do not introduce the dropper as far as the ear canal, but instead massage the ear gently to encourage the liquid medication to disperse inwards. And if you suspect that a foreign object, perhaps a grass seed, has become lodged in your feline's ear, its extraction should be left to your vet. Because the symptoms of many ear afflictions are so similar, an accurate home diagnosis can be difficult to make, so take your cat to the vet's if you suspect that it is suffering from any of the following.

CLEAN A CAT'S EAR WITH MOISTENED COTTON WOOL.

as enabling you to identify the source of the problem better, wiping the inside of your cat's ear flaps with a wad of cotton wool soaked in warm water often proves a helpful initial hygiene measure. Never, however, insert a finger, cotton bud, tweezers or any other object into your cat's ear canal as the consequences in

Symptoms

- Ear-scratching, head-shaking and brown discharge within the ear: see ear mites and outer-ear infection.
- Blood blister on an ear flap: see aural haematoma.
- Flaky, red skin or sores around the edges of the ear flap: see sunburn.
- Tilting of the head and a wobbly gait: see middle- and inner-ear infections.
- Lack of response to sounds: see deafness.

Ear mites

Sometimes also called ear canker or otodectic
mange, an infestation of ear mites (*Otodectes
cynotis*) occurs within the feline ear canal and is
spread by contact with an infested animal, not
always another feline. Kittens are particularly
prone to the unwelcome attentions of these tiny
white mites, and the danger signs include
repeated ear-scratching, in extreme cases
sometimes causing hair loss and bleeding, and
head-shaking as the cat tries to rid itself of the
excruciating irritation that is caused by the
mites' aggravating presence. On closer
examination, you will usually see – and,
perhaps, smell – a reddish-brown, waxy
discharge and possibly encrustation, the ear's
defensive response to chronic irritation and the
signal that you should take your cat to the vet's.
If the diagnosis is confirmed by a sighting of the
mites under a magnifying torch, the vet will
usually first clean the cat's ears thoroughly and
then give you some ear drops with which to
eradicate them over a period of a few weeks.
Although they aren't blood-suckers, instead
deriving nourishment from feline earwax, don't
ignore an infestation of ear mites because not
only would you be prolonging your cat's distress
if you did so, but a bacterial infection could
subsequently set in.

Aural haematoma

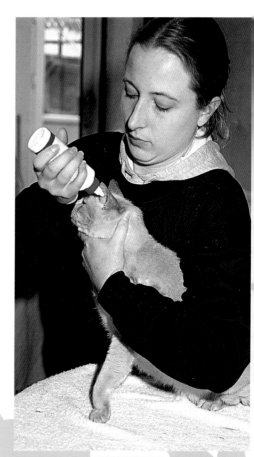

EAR DROPS ALLEVIATE MANY AURAL AFFLICTIONS.

Typically seen on the outside of a cat's ear flap,
a blood blister, or haematoma, results from
either a cat fight or from the feline repeatedly,
and forcibly, scratching at an irritated area,
causing the blood vessels on the surface of the

skin to burst and the released blood to be trapped between the ear's cartilage and epidermis. There are two reasons why you should seek the vet's attention: firstly, because it is more than likely that the underlying cause of the cat's scratching is chronic and needs to be addressed and, secondly, because as the blood within the blister slowly disperses, it may cause a distortion evocatively named 'flop ear' (or sometimes the 'cauliflower ear' notorious to boxers), which is why the vet may take the precaution of draining away the blood and may also prescribe antibiotics to ward off infection.

Sunburn

As unlikely as it may seem, white or light-coloured cats are susceptible to sunburn. Because their skins are scarcely pigmented, and because the tips and edges of their ears aren't protected by a dense layer of fur, these areas, along with the nose and eyelids, are the most typically damaged by the sun's powerful, ultraviolet rays. If you notice that one, or both, of your cat's ear flaps are rimmed with red, flaky skin, and especially if you know that it enjoys sun-bathing, consult your vet for confirmation that it is suffering from sunburn. Although the damage progresses slowly, the flaking skin may be replaced by sores, scabs,

YOUR VET MAY PRESCRIBE A SOOTHING PREPARATION.

ulcers and ultimately full-blown squamous-cell carcinoma, a destructive form of cancer that may require the ear to be amputated if allowed to spread. If you are vigilant, however, it shouldn't reach this stage, and you should prevent it from doing so either by keeping your cat out of the sun or by applying sunblock formulated for children to the most vulnerable parts of its body.

205

Outer-ear infection

If, during a grooming session, you notice a pungent-smelling, brown, waxy discharge within your cat's ear, it is likely that it has either been infested with ear mites (see above) or, more seriously, and particularly if the discharge contains pus, that a bacterial or fungal infection (sometimes called by the Latin designation otitis externa) has taken hold. In order to prevent the condition worsening and causing irreparable damage, as well as to put a stop to any discomfort or pain that your feline may be enduring, it's important to take your cat to the vet's as soon as you can. If an outer-ear infection is diagnosed, you'll be given the appropriate anti-bacterial or -fungal medication to administer at home.

Middle- and inner-ear infections

If neglected, an infection of the outer ear, whatever the cause, may spread inwards, into the middle ear, dangerously close to the vestibular organ that controls the feline sense of balance (see page 44) in the inner ear. Although you may not detect a middle- or inner-ear infection from the presence of discharge, if your normally agile cat becomes wobbly on its feet, staggers around in a circle (the direction identifying the infected ear) or its sense of balance otherwise appears to have been compromised, warning bells should start ringing. Further symptoms of a middle- or inner-ear infection include intermittent deafness and the cat – which will be starting to suffer considerable pain and distress – constantly tilting its head to one side. Take your profoundly disoriented cat to the veterinary surgery without delay, where any deep-seated discharge may be drained away and a course of powerful medication prescribed. Time is of the essence if nerve damage and permanent deafness are to be avoided.

Deafness

Although it may sometimes be caused by a middle- or inner-ear infection, white cats with blue eyes, in which deafness is a genetic defect, and older cats are at risk of losing their sense of hearing. Just as in humans, deafness in felines manifests itself as a lack of response to sounds, which is unusual in creatures whose sense of hearing is exceptionally acute. Since hearing aids are not available for cats, there is nothing that can be done except to make sure that your cat's deafness does not expose it to danger. Confinement to the home or a securely fenced garden may therefore be advisable to ensure that your cat, who may not hear a car approaching, does not fall victim to a road traffic accident.

Afflictions of the eyes

Many feline eye problems, which often stem from scratches inflicted during cat fights, are both relatively insignificant and easily cleared up with the correct treatment, but, as with any physical malfunction, mustn't be neglected in case an infection blows up and the eyesight is threatened. Other eye afflictions, however, are potentially very serious, and because the similarity of the symptoms that indicate that all is not well with a feline eye can make it difficult for you to identify a condition correctly, it's essential that the diagnosis is made by a vet, who will also advise you on the appropriate remedial action.

A CAT'S BRIGHT EYES MAY SUCCUMB TO CERTAIN OCULAR AFFLICTIONS.

It almost goes without saying that a feline's eyes are extremely sensitive, so always treat them with the utmost delicacy and never poke anything into them, even a gentle finger. As part of its treatment, your vet may, however, advise you to bathe your cat's eyes with either warm water or a feline-specific ocular preparation – don't use eye drops formulated for human use – in which case do so by gently pressing a pad of cotton wool generously soaked in the liquid against the afflicted (closed) eye. Although an eye bath will temporarily soothe the irritation and may expedite the removal of a foreign body, your cat probably won't appreciate this procedure, so be warned that you may have to pre-empt it struggling by swaddling its body in a towel so that only its head protrudes. The same advice applies if you've been instructed to apply

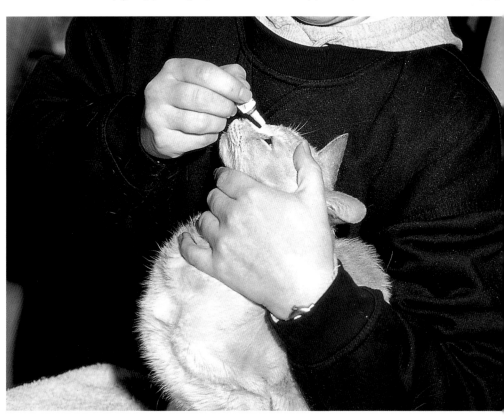

APPLYING CREAM TO A CAT'S EYE

a feline eye ointment, which you should squeeze along the lower eyelid before closing both lids and gently massaging the eye.

CAUTION! A CAT'S EYES ARE EXTREMELY SENSITIVE.

Symptoms

- Clear tears running from the eye: see blocked tear ducts.
- Pawing at the eye: see foreign bodies.
- Repeated blinking or a half- or fully closed eye: see scratched cornea and conjunctivitis.
- The third-eyelid pulled over the eye: see haw problems.
- Turned-in eyelids: see entropion.
- Cloudy discharge from the eye: see conjunctivitis.
- A swollen, unblinking eye: see glaucoma.
- An opaque eye: see glaucoma and cataract.
- Bumping into obstacles and a lack of response to movement: see blindness.

Blocked tear ducts

Being unsentimental creatures, felines don't cry, so if your cat appears to be weeping, the discharge is clear and it seems otherwise fit and well, its tear ducts are probably blocked.

Although you could give its eye, along with the affected fur beneath, a preliminary bathing with warm water (see above), you should still seek your vet's expert opinion as soon as you are able in case further treatment is needed.

Foreign bodies

You'll usually be alerted to the presence of a foreign body in a cat's eye if it is obviously, and repeatedly, pawing at the affected eye, an action that felines otherwise never demonstrate, even when grooming their faces. Immediate inspection of the problem eye is required, and if the object is on the surface of the eyeball, you may be able to dislodge it by bathing the eye (see above). Do not attempt this if the foreign body has penetrated the surface of the eye, however, in case you cause serious damage, and instead whisk your cat to the vet's for immediate attention.

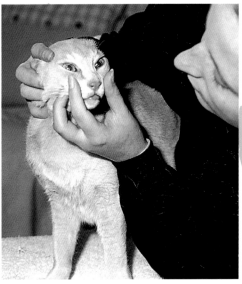

CHECK EYES FOR SIGNS OF FOREIGN BODIES

Scratched cornea

If your cat is either blinking constantly (which cats rarely do) or keeping one of its eyelids closed or half-closed, it is probably doing so because its eyeball is sore, usually due to either a scratched cornea or an infection. By lowering its eyelid, the cat is attempting to protect its painful eye from the drying effect of the air and to soothe the irritation with a film of moisture.

The first step is to bathe the eye, as detailed above, and then to consult the vet to prevent an infection, and ultimately possibly ulceration, from taking hold.

Haw problems

When a cat is sleeping, it sometimes does so with its eyes open, but with the haws – commonly known as the third eyelids, but more properly as the nictitating membranes – pulled across them to provide protection. This is quite normal, but if a haw, which is usually retracted and tucked into the inner corner of the wakeful eye, is visible when the cat is going about its everyday business, it may indicate damage, either to the haw or to the eye beneath, or more general illness. If only one haw is visible, the problem will typically be confined to that eye; if both are pulled across each eye, however, the cat may be sickening for something serious, such as feline viral rhinotracheitis, one of the viruses implicated in feline infectious respiratory disease (see page 144). If the condition persists for longer than a day, consult your vet for a diagnosis and the appropriate treatment.

Entropion

Entropion, or rolled-in eyelids, may either be a congenital condition (common to Persians) or the result of a chronic eye inflammation. Because it causes constant discomfort and irritation, your vet may advise surgical correction, which is often the only cure.

Conjunctivitis

The symptoms described above for a scratched cornea, accompanied by visible inflammation of the eye and, more tellingly, by cloudy discharge, often signal conjunctivitis induced by a chronic allergy or a bacterial or viral infection, such as feline infectious respiratory disease, and specifically feline viral rhinotracheitis (see page 144). Any eye infection must be treated as soon as possible lest it develops into an irreversible, sight-threatening condition, so waste no time in presenting your cat to the vet.

Glaucoma

If one of your cat's eyes appears to be swollen – perhaps so much so that it cannot close its eyelids – and the eye itself looks cloudy or glassy, the situation is serious. It may be that your cat has suffered a blow to the head, causing internal bleeding, or that it has a grave infection or a tumour, all of which can cause glaucoma, a condition in which the aqueous humour within the eye is unable to circulate freely, resulting in a dangerous build-up of pressure. Often also associated with old age, glaucoma can ultimately result in some extreme scenarios, including blindness, and, if at all, can only be treated by the vet, who may deem it necessary to remove the afflicted eye.

Cataract

In common with their human counterparts, feline senior citizens, and also diabetic cats, may develop cataracts within the lenses of their eyes, which can be identified by the presence of a white film or white pupil. Although there is no danger of infection, a cataract can cause progressive loss of sight and an increased danger of glaucoma, so seek your vet's advice about having it removed, which may be advocated if cataracts are affecting both of the cat's eyes and hence significantly impairing its vision.

211

Blindness

If your normally sure-footed feline starts to bump into obstacles or doesn't respond to rapid movements, it may be that it can no longer see them. One way of checking is to sit your cat on a table and then gently to cover each eye in turn with one hand while moving an outstretched finger of the other towards its open eye. If it blinks, it has registered the movement, but if it remains unmoved, loss of sight is indicated. On closer examination, your vet should be able to determine the cause, which,

A CAT'S NOSE INDICATES ITS GENERAL HEALTH.

depending on the diagnosis, may mean that its blindness is only temporary and that its eyesight can be restored, as is sometimes the case if the cause is neurological or a cataract, for example. If, however, its loss of sight is permanent, you'll have to keep your vision-impaired cat inside for the rest of its life and

ensure that the position of its bed, litter tray, food and water bowls – and preferably the furniture, too – is never changed so that it does not suffer the anxiety of not being able to locate these familiar components of its everyday life.

Afflictions of the nose

Caspar once alarmed us – and himself – by suddenly developing a runny nose a few weeks after his booster immunisation and shortly after a further routine trip to the vet's. Because this is a potentially serious sign, we rushed him back to see the vet, whose diagnosis was that, in the absence of any other symptoms and, as sometimes happens when felines are under stress, the second, anxiety-inducing visit had caused the active agents within the vaccine temporarily to surface. After a week of precautionary antibiotics, all was well. Caspar, however, who was obviously unable to clutch a handkerchief, had a most unpleasant time mopping up the stream from his nose with his tongue, despite being aided every so often by a human wiping his nose with cotton wool dampened with warm water. (Although it wasn't necessary for us to do this, note that you can temporarily ease any soreness caused by chronic mucus production by smearing a light layer of petroleum jelly over a cat's nose.)

Because we'd been vigilant about maintaining Caspar's immunisation programme, we knew that it was unlikely that he was suffering from a full-blown case of feline viral rhinotracheitis, one of the viruses that goes under the umbrella name of feline infectious respiratory disease (see page 144), but if your cat has a runny nose and its immunity to this serious illness is questionable, cat flu may be a chilling possibility. Another cause may be a localised infection. In both instances, urgent veterinary treatment will be required, to take your cat to the vet's as soon as you can.

Other internal nasal problems include irritation caused by an allergy or a blockage within the nose, when, as in all instances of nasal problems, you should consult your vet immediately. Inhalation treatment may be advocated, in which case follow the vet's instructions. Never squirt a nasal decongestant formulated for humans up a cat's nose, however, and never try to remove a foreign object from a feline's nose yourself.

External nasal problems include sunburn (see page 205) and scratches inflicted during fights, both of which should be carefully monitored to ensure that they do not develop into chronic conditions, at the same time as keeping the

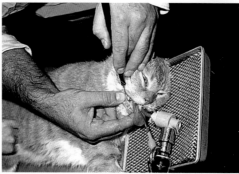

SCALING REQUIRES A CAT TO BE ANAESTHETISED.

cat's nose clean by regularly wiping it with water-soaked cotton wool.

Afflictions of the mouth

Whereas Caspar's episode of nasal distress was immediately apparent to us, I'm ashamed to say that we had no idea that Melchior was suffering from the onset of localised dental disease until the vet discovered two affected teeth during a routine check-up. Although the condition was not advanced, it could only worsen, eventually leading to the collapse of the teeth concerned and possible infection, so Melchior was anaesthetised, the decaying teeth were extracted and his remaining teeth were scaled (Caspar didn't escape the anaesthetisation-and-scaling procedure either). That was many years ago, and since then our felines have had to put up with having their teeth brushed weekly (see page 117 for equipment and page 173 for

guidelines), partly as result of which they can now boast excellent dental health.

Whether or not you brush your cat's teeth, it's important to look inside your cat's mouth as a matter of routine to check for any problems that may be brewing within its gums, mouth lining and tongue. Signs that a condition has become chronic include bad breath, drooling and obvious pain when eating – or even a disinclination to eat – but it's clearly better to pre-empt the development of these secondary symptoms by monitoring your cat's dental health. Many ailments of the mouth, teeth and gums are both minor and curable, but others may indicate a significant threat to your feline's health, so consult your vet if any of the symptoms listed below are giving you cause for concern.

Symptoms

- Bad breath and a layer of yellow or grey material on the top of the teeth: see tartar.
- Red, inflamed gums: see gingivitis.
- Pale gums: see anaemia.
- A swollen cheek and inflamed gum: see abscess.
- A sore on the inside of the upper lip: see rodent ulcer.
- Sores on the tongue or gums: see mouth ulcers.
- A swelling under the tongue: see ranula.

Tartar

Although tooth-eroding sugar isn't to blame for feline dental decay, unlike among humans, the high calcium content of most cats' diets can result in this nutrient being deposited on their teeth. Furthermore, because many house cats subsist on soft, tinned food, there the deposits may remain to calcify, in contrast to their feral fellows, which scrape the deposits away while devouring the tough bodies of their prey. (Note that dried food may therefore be better than

MOUTH PROBLEMS

tinned for your feline's dental health; alternatively, give it a chewy or tooth-friendly treat every so often.) It's best to brush your cat's teeth at least once a week to prevent the build-up of tartar (dental calculus), an accumulation of which will require your cat to be anaesthetised to enable the vet to remove it by scaling. If your cat's breath smells bad, examine its teeth to see if they are covered with a layer of tartar, which, if left untreated, could result in gingevitis, progressing to periodontal disease.

Gingivitis

If your cat's gums look red and sore, it is probably suffering from gingivitis, an inflammation of the gums caused by a build-up at the neck of the teeth of tartar and plaque, bacteria-harbouring food deposits. Chronic gingivitis is indicated when the gums are severely swollen and prone to bleeding. Unless the condition is addressed, it may advance to become periodontal disease, whereby infection sets in and attacks the tissues and bone surrounding the teeth, ultimately causing their destabilisation, death of the dental nerves and hence also of the teeth, which will then need to be extracted. It's therefore vital that you act as soon as you see the danger signs, preferably in the earliest stages of the condition, when only a

thin red line along the part of the gum immediately adjoining the teeth will be visible.

Anaemia

Feline gums should be rosy pink in colour, but if they appear unusually pale, and the cat hasn't suffered a shock, anaemia is indicated, especially if the feline seems listless. This debilitating condition is caused by a reduction in either the red blood cells or a dilution of haemoglobin within the blood, and may be a symptom of feline leukaemia (see page 145). Take your cat to the vet's for diagnosis and treatment as soon as possible.

Abscess

An abscess may be caused when an infection has taken hold in the root of a damaged tooth, resulting in widespread swelling and inflammation and causing the cat exquisite pain when pressure is applied – for example, while eating – when its distress will be obvious. The usual remedy is for the vet to extract the problem tooth and to prescribe a course of antibiotics with which to clear up the underlying infection and hence abscess.

Rodent ulcer

By pawing at its mouth, your cat may be unwittingly alerting you to an irritating mouth

condition, and if it seems to be targeting its
upper lip, gently roll the lip back to investigate
further. If you can see a sore, it may be a
rodent ulcer (eosinophilic granuloma), which,
although not in itself especially serious, is likely
to persist, to your cat's distress, if not subjected
to veterinary treatment.

Mouth ulcers

Sores on the tongue or gums may be
symptomatic either of local irritation or else of
the more threatening feline infectious respiratory
disease (see page 144) or kidney disease
(caused by increased levels of ammonia within
the saliva), both of which require the urgent
attention of your vet.

Ranula

You should always investigate the inside of
your cat's mouth if it seems to be suffering
discomfort when eating, and if you then see a
translucent swelling under its tongue, it's likely
to be a ranula, a fluid-filled cyst that is formed
when the saliva ducts become blocked or
damaged. Ranulas generally respond well to
veterinary treatment.

Monitoring a cat's vital signs

Whether or not your cat has developed any
worrying symptoms, if it doesn't seem itself and

you are concerned about its health, monitoring
its vital signs may help you to decide whether
you should take it to the vet's. Although the
vet's first step would be to take its temperature,
you would be emphatically advised against
doing so yourself unless you are experienced in
the procedure and also possess the correct type
of thermometer. To explain further, the
temperature-sensitive strips that you can place
across a child's forehead are useless when it
comes to felines, as is putting a digital or glass
thermometer in its mouth and telling it to keep
still for a minute or two. The only accurate way
of gauging a cat's temperature is to insert a
thermometer designed especially for animals
into its rectum (the cat may struggle against this
indignity, causing a human-specific thermometer

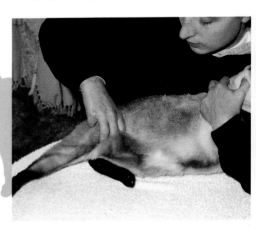

**YOU CAN FEEL A CAT'S PULSE BEAT AT A CERTAIN
POINT WHERE THE BACK LEG MEETS THE TORSO.**

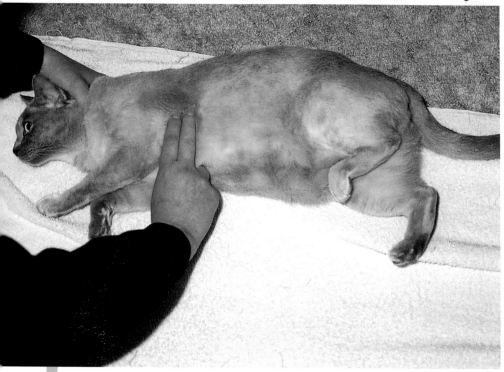

GENTLY PLACING TWO FINGERS OVER A CAT'S HEART ENABLES YOU TO JUDGE THE STRENGTH OF ITS HEARTBEAT.

to break and internal damage to be wreaked). Although taking a cat's temperature should therefore be left to the vet, for the record, a cat's normal temperature is between 38 and 38.6°C (100.4 and 101.5°F), a higher reading therefore indicating infection or illness, although if a cat is feeling stressed, a slightly higher reading may also result (as always happens when Caspar, who has no particular reason that we can discern for his anxiety, finds himself in the veterinary surgery, another obvious manifestation of his uneasiness being 'stress-moulting', the rapid shedding of hairs).

What you can safely do, however, is check your cat's pulse by holding your finger against the inside of its 'thigh', the spot where the back leg adjoins the torso, where the femoral artery runs close to the skin's surface, for thirty seconds (it may help to ask someone else to act as a time-keeper so that you can concentrate on taking the pulse).

feline afflictions

Count the pulse beats as you feel them and then, when the thirty seconds are up, double the total so that you obtain a per-minute figure. The normal pulse rate for an unstressed cat ranges between 110 and 140 beats a minute. If the cat seemed agitated as a result of having been restrained, you can probably discount a slightly higher rate, but if it appeared calm or apathetic, a significantly higher, weak or erratic pulse should be taken as a signal to take it to the vet's as soon possible – your cat could be really ill – for further investigation and remedial treatment.

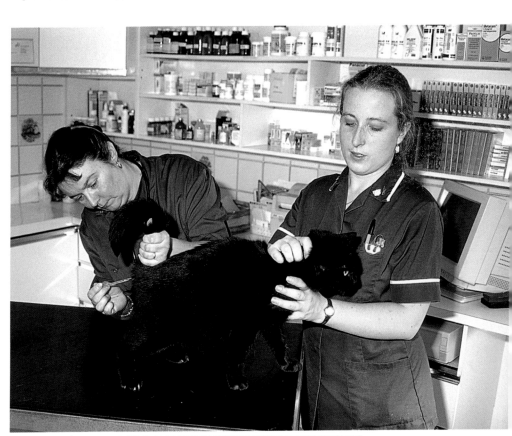

TAKING A CAT'S TEMPERATURE IS A JOB THAT IS BEST LEFT TO THE PROFESSIONALS.

Giving a cat medication

If the vet has prescribed medication for your cat, you will have to perfect the art of administering it, both to ensure that it has the desired effect and to avoid distressing your feline patient through your clumsiness. While the recommended procedures for administering eye preparations and ear drops (see pages 208 to 209 and 203) have already been covered, and applying ointment to the skin is a straightforward process (always wash your hands afterwards), those for giving internal medication – powders, pills and their liquid counterparts – will be made easier with the help of a little insider know-how.

Introducing powdered medication into the feline body is relatively easy: if it is mixed into a ball with a little of your cat's favourite fresh food, such as tuna, it will usually be readily swallowed without your cat realising the deception.

Although it becomes automatic with practice, the first few times that you give a cat a pill, you'll probably find the process tricky, not least because you may have to restrain your protesting cat with one hand and administer the pill with the other. You may therefore find it easier either to lift the cat onto a table and ask someone gently to hold its front legs and restrain its rear end or to wrap it in a towel so that only its head protrudes. See the following pages for further instructions on administering pills and liquid medication.

If any medication that isn't intended to make the cat vomit has this effect, discontinue the treatment and consult your vet, as it may be that your cat is allergic to it. And if you have difficulty giving your cat medication, ask your vet for a demonstration.

Administering Medicine

1 With your feline immobilised, encircle its jaw with one hand, so that your thumb and forefinger are on either side of its mouth, and tilt its head backwards.

2 Now apply a little pressure with your thumb and forefinger (alternatively, gently push down on the lower jaw using the index finger of your other hand) until its mouth opens and then, using your free hand, quickly pop the pill as far to the back of its mouth as you can. (You could use a pill dispenser, or 'popper', rather than your fingers, but don't push the tube too far into the cat's mouth in case you damage its delicate interior).

3 *Finally, close the cat's mouth and hold it shut with one hand while stroking its throat with the other to encourage it to swallow its medication. Only then release your hold, but watch your feline to ensure that it has actually swallowed the pill and doesn't instead spit it out (lip-licking is a sure sign that the pill has gone done).*

4 *If you're administering liquid medication, use a dropper (preferably a plastic one, not glass, in case the cat bites and shatters it) or a syringe and either introduce the liquid in the same way as you would a pill or hold the cat's mouth shut with one hand and inject the liquid into the space behind a canine tooth. The medication should be administered a drop at a time to prevent your cat from choking on a flood of liquid. In both instances, when you're done, again keep the cat's mouth closed and stroke its throat until it swallows its medicine.*

221

Caring for an injured or sick cat

There may be occasions when you have to provide more dedicated nursing care than simply administering medication: for example, if your cat's skin has suffered significant damage as a result of infestation, infection or injury, in which case your vet may advocate a bandage or an Elizabethan collar. A feline who has succumbed to a serious illness, however, may require more devoted nursing to encourage it to recover its health and strength.

Although the following general tips may prove helpful, you must obey your vet's instructions to the letter to ensure that your cat receives the care that it badly needs following a severe physical trauma.

Bandages and Elizabethan collars

Because a feline's flesh repairs itself remarkably quickly following an injury, it is not usually necessary to bandage any scratches or superficial wounds that your cat may sustain. The exceptions are, however, if it persistently licks or scratches at a skin injury, thereby both retarding the healing process and introducing the risk of infection, or if the wound is so large or deep that it could be infected as it heals. If your vet has instructed you to apply an ointment, your cat may furthermore lick it off, in which case you may need to enlist the help of a bandage (and the gauze, crêpe and cotton bandages sold for human use are also fine for use on felines).

A tail can be bandaged in the same way as a paw or leg, but a wound to the abdomen will require a body bandage. Your vet will advise you how to make, or obtain, one of these and also, if it is advocated, how to bandage a cat's eye or ear.

If your cat is suffering from a chronically itchy or inflamed patch of skin, particularly anywhere on its head, your vet may recommend that it wears an Elizabethan collar — a forward-pointing, funnel-shaped contraption resembling an Elizabethan ruff that is secured around the neck — to prevent it from licking, pawing or scratching at its skin before it's healed. Keep your cat inside for the duration because your feline's temporarily limited field of vision may endanger its safety. The collar may be removed occasionally to enable the cat to eat, drink, groom itself and use the litter try without hindrance, but as soon as it shows any signs of turning its attention to the affected area, it's time to replace its collar.

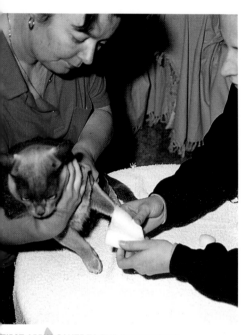

FIRST APPLY GAUZE TO THE INJURED AREA.

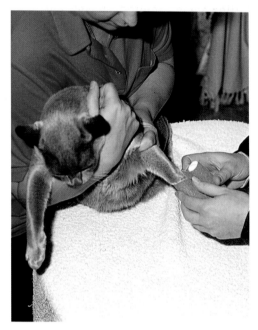

WRAP THE PAW IN COTTON WOOL, THEN BEGIN TO BANDAGE.

Before bandaging your cat, gently wash the affected skin with cotton wool soaked in dilute saline (salt) solution and then, if the vet's advised you to do so, apply ointment before reaching for a clean piece of gauze.

When bandaging a paw or leg, first apply the gauze, then wrap the paw in cotton wool and finally commence bandaging, working from the foot up the leg and overlapping each turn that you make. The cat won't welcome being swaddled in a bandage, which it will regard as an alien irritant and will often try to remove, so it's important that the bandage is neither loose enough to unravel easily, nor so tight that it impairs the circulation. Never secure the end of a bandage with a safety pin, which could spring open and prick the cat, or tie it off in case the cat worries at the knot with its teeth, thereby causing the bandage to unravel. Instead use a strong sticking plaster, one end of which should be applied to the fur above to keep the bandage in place (when it's time to remove it, don't pull it off, but cut it away with a pair of scissors).

Nursing a sick feline

During, and following, an episode of serious injury or illness, your vet may advise you to supplement any prescription medication with round-the-clock nursing to aid your cat's recovery. This involves confining the patient to bed (which, because your cat will be probably be feeling abnormally weak, shouldn't present a problem) in a dim, warm and quiet spot. Make sure that the bed is as comfortable as possible, but use only disposable or washable bedding, which, for the sake of cleanliness, should be changed regularly, especially if the invalid is incontinent. If the patient is unable to stand up, reposition its body every few hours to prevent pressure sores from developing.

A SICK FELINE REQUIRES PLENTY OF REST.

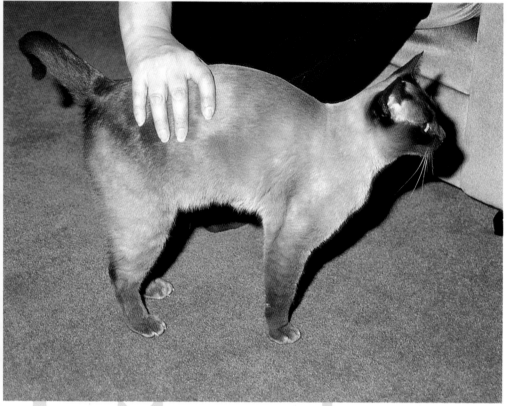

YOUR CAT MAY NEED SOME HELP WITH GETTING AROUND, AS WELL AS LOTS OF TENDER LOVING CARE.

Place the litter tray nearby, but note that if your cat is simply too weak to reach it, you may have to lift it into the tray two or three times a day. Leave a bowl of fresh water next to the patient's bed, too, and give it small portions of its favourite food as often as it will accept them (see page 166 for advice on how to tempt a sick or old cat to eat). If the cat can't, or won't, eat, your vet will usually deem it necessary for you to give it liquidised food (ask for advice on what best to feed it) through a syringe, in which case you should follow the same procedure as described for administering liquid medication (see page 221).

It's important to maintain an ill cat's morale, and little makes a fastidious feline feel more depressed than being dirty. So if these parts of

225

your cat's body need cleaning, bathe its nose, lips or eyes in a very dilute mixture of salt and water, dry them off gently and finally, if they are sore or cracked, smear a little petroleum jelly – but use a prescription ointment for the eyes – over them. An inflamed rear end or soiled fur should first be cleansed with mild shampoo diluted in warm water and then dried and dressed with a little petroleum jelly. Finally, lightly and carefully comb or brush the invalid's coat. (Remember always to wash your hands after cleaning or handling a feline patient.)

A sick cat will be reassured by your attention and affection – tending to a feline's psychological state can be as important as ministering to its physical well-being – so spend some time talking to it soothingly, but don't make too much of a fuss of it because rest is vital to its recovery. And if all goes well, the care that you and your vet have given it will enable your invalid slowly to recover, and one of the first signs that it is on the mend will be when it starts trying to wash its face.

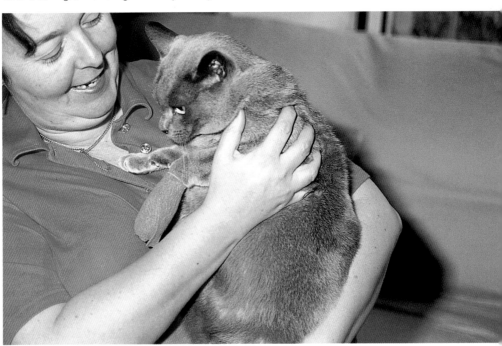

YOUR CAT WILL NEED PLENTY OF ATTENTION IF IT IS SICK OR INJURED.

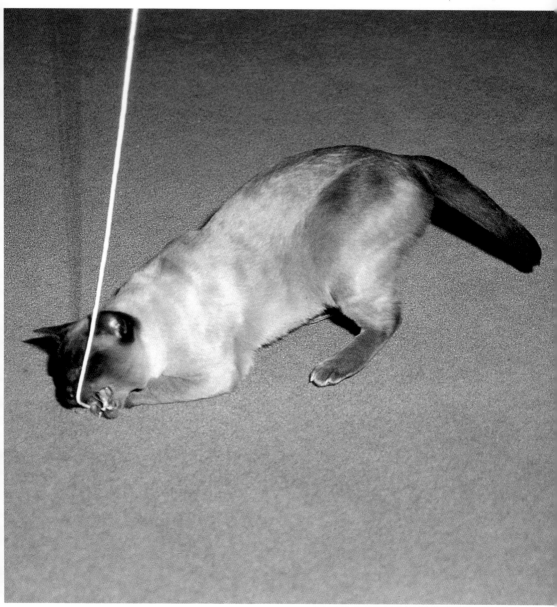

WITH CARE AND LOVE, YOUR CAT SHOULD SOON BE AS HIGH - SPIRITED AS EVER!

5

Symptom diagnosis and emergency action

If your cat has developed a physical problem, it will usually alert you to both its presence and cause by a change in its behaviour: if a feline repeatedly scratches its skin, for instance, a number of underlying irritants may be implicated, as outlined in Chapter 4. This chapter highlights the symptoms that may warn of a potentially serious threat to a feline's health, as well as outlining the emergency action to take should your cat suffer one of a number of accidents that could endanger its life.

Although the following pages will help you to identify the problem and, in the case of an accident, advise you on initial first-aid treatment, always rush an ailing or injured cat to the vet's as soon as possible. In many cases, it is only prompt veterinary expertise and attention that can save a feline's life.

CHECKING FOR SYMPTOMS

Symptom diagnosis

The following sections delineate some of the symptoms that may point towards a possibly grave condition that will require veterinary treatment; others, however, may be minor or temporary symptoms and problems. Some of these conditions have already been covered where indicated, and where an asterisk appears, refer to the emergency-action section for guidance on initial treatment.

Although they have been presented separately, some symptoms may occur in combination – vomiting and diarrhoea, for instance – so don't consider them in isolation, especially if your cat seems listless, has lost its appetite or otherwise doesn't seem its usual self.

Writing down a list of your cat's symptoms before taking it to the veterinary surgery will both help you to remember them and give the vet valuable information on which to act.

If your feline doesn't appear unduly bothered by a symptom, wait for twenty-four hours to see if it clears up (vomiting for example, may simply be caused by having swallowed a number of hairs, by having eaten too much or too quickly or by having ingested something that disagrees with the cat's digestion), but if it persists thereafter, take it to the vet's.

Finally, while you should never ignore a chronic symptom, don't be too alarmed by the doom-and-gloom pictures that the following lists may paint and remember that if they are addressed in time, many of these symptoms can be halted in their tracks: Caspar, for example, has suffered bouts of both colitis and cystitis in the past, but, following the appropriate veterinary treatment, has made a full recovery and is today free of both conditions.

A CAT WILL USUALLY ALERT YOU TO A PROBLEM.

Lumps and bumps

Hard, throbbing, pus-filled lump: abscess*.

Soft, fluid-filled swelling: cyst.

Soft, blood-filled swelling: haematoma; see also aural haematoma (pages 204 to 205).

A number of hard nodules: fungal infection, feline leprosy.

Tumour: benign or malignant growth; see also feline leukaemia (page 145).

Mobility problems

Lack of co-ordination: poisoning*, feline infectious peritonitis, eclampsia (in mother cats), stroke; see also feline panleucopenia (page 143).

Trembling: shock, poisoning*, hypothermia, neurological disorder.

Twitching and spasms: poisoning*, eclampsia (in mother cats), tetanus.

Staggering: poisoning*, injury, concussion, eclampsia (in mother cats), encephalitis; see also middle- and inner-ear infections (page 206).

Fits* or convulsions: poisoning*, calcium or thiamine (vitamin B1) deficiency, infection, head injury, epilepsy, meningitis, feline infectious peritonitis, brain tumour, hepatitis, nephritis (kidney disease), hypoglycaemia (diabetes), eclampsia (in mother cats).

Limping or stiffness: injury (sprain, fracture), foreign body in the paw, bone infection, rickets, vitamin A poisoning, tumour, nephritis, cystitis, tetanus, arthritis, rheumatism, inflamed or dislocated joint, spinal damage.

Stiff neck: vitamin A poisoning.

Swollen leg or paw: injury (sprain, fracture), infection, abscess*, tumour, arthritis, oedema (dropsy), inflamed or dislocated joint.

Paralysis: injury, concussion, poisoning*, iliac thrombosis, stroke, encephalitis, brain tumour, spinal damage, tetanus.

Respiratory problems

Chronic sneezing: allergic reaction to airborne pollutants, asthma; see also feline infectious respiratory disease (page 144).

Wheezing: bronchial asthma, heart disease, lungworms.

Coughing: foreign body stuck in the throat, allergic reaction to airborne pollutants, growths in the mouth or throat; bronchitis, heart disease, lungworms, heartworms; see also worms (pages 146 to 148), feline infectious respiratory disease (page 144).

Catarrh: fungal infection; see also feline infectious respiratory disease (page 144).

Abnormal breathing patterns: heatstroke, hypothermia, shock, poisoning*, foreign body stuck in the nose, asthma, injury of the lung or chest, fungal infection, bronchitis, pneumonia, pleurisy, heart disease, anaemia, post-partum haemorrhage or eclampsia (in mother cats); see also feline infectious respiratory disease and feline leukaemia (pages 144 and 145).

Urinary problems

Chronic thirst: poisoning*, gastritis, enteritis, diabetes, nephritis, hepatitis, pyometra or puerperal metritis (in mother cats); see also feline panleucopenia (page 143).

Increased urination or urinary incontinence: psychological unsettlement, nephritis, old age, diabetes, urethral infection or damage, hormonal imbalance (in females), neurological or spinal damage.

Bleeding from the penis: bladder infection.

Blood-tinged urine: injury, urinary-tract blockage or infection, nephritis, cystitis.

Straining when urinating: urinary-tract blockage or infection, cystitis, calculi (or urolithias, urinary-tract stones).

Gastric and bowel problems

Abnormal eating patterns: increased need for nourishment, diabetes; see also worms (pages 146 to 148) and feline leukaemia (page 145).

Drooling: foreign body stuck in the throat, mouth affliction, heatstroke, poisoning*, ulcerative glossitis, fits* or convulsions; see also feline infectious respiratory disease (page 144).

Vomiting: furballs, indigestion, gastritis, enteritis, poisoning*, feline infectious peritonitis, feline dysautonomia (Key-Gaskell syndrome), hepatitis, pancreatitis, nephritis, diabetes, puerperal metritis, pyometra or eclampsia (in mother cats), intestinal blockage, constipation; see also worms (pages 146 to 148), feline panleucopenia, feline infectious respiratory disease and feline leukaemia (pages 143 to 145).

Abdominal pain: constipation, poisoning*, feline infectious peritonitis, enteritis, hepatitis, nephritis, calculi (or urolithias, urinary-tract stones), pancreatitis, puerperal metritis (in mother cats), intestinal blockage; see also feline panleucopenia (page 143).

Diarrhoea: food intolerance, stress, gastritis, enteritis, feline infectious peritonitis, hepatitis, spinal damage; see also worms (pages 146 to 148), feline panleucopenia and feline leukaemia (pages 143 and 145).

Blood or mucus in the faeces: constipation, colitis, enteritis; see also feline panleucopenia (page 143).

Constipation: lack of water and a dry diet, furballs, intestinal blockage, rectal prolapse, liver disease, feline dysautonomia (Key-Gaskell syndrome), loss of muscular tone in older cats, lack of exercise, spinal damage; see also worms (pages 146 to 148).

Anal irritation: blocked anal glands; see also worms (page 146 to 148), maggots and eczema and dermatitis (pages 200 and 201).

Emergency action

If, despite all of your safety precautions, the worst comes to the worst and your cat has an accident or another type of life-threatening encounter, the following reference section may prove helpful in giving it emergency treatment. Once you have stabilised its condition, however, you should immediately phone the vet for further advice and instructions. Thereafter, you'll probably be asked to take it to the vet's at once for expert remedial – even life-saving – treatment.

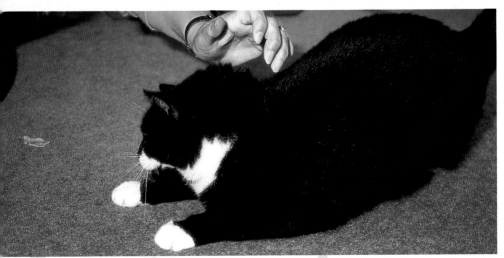

GIVE A TRAUMATISED CAT SOME GENTLE REASSURANCE.

Although a traumatised feline will probably not in any case be interested in eating or drinking, do not offer it any food or water in case a pre-operative general anaesthetic is required. Remember, too, that a cat that has met with any kind of mishap will be terrified by what has befallen it, so try to stay calm in case you drive it into an even greater state of panic, talk to it soothingly and reassuringly and handle it with the utmost gentleness.

A final word of caution: never give your cat an aspirin: despite its status as a human panacea, aspirin has a toxic effect on the feline body and may cause irreversible liver damage.

Scratches, minor cuts and puncture wounds

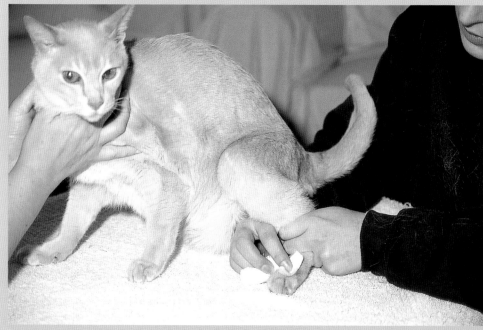

DISINFECT A SKIN WOUND WITH COTTON WOOL DIPPED IN SALINE SOLUTION.

If a cat has suffered at the teeth or claws of another feline, it's important to disinfect the wound because the injured cat will inevitable lick it, thereby introducing infection-inducing bacteria and increasing the danger of an abscess developing. The same applies to minor cuts inflicted, perhaps, by a splinter of glass or a thorn (if it is still embedded in the skin, remove it with a pair of tweezers). Puncture wounds caused by claws or teeth, and even deep scratches, rarely bleed for long, and once the bleeding has stopped, if necessary clip away the surrounding hair and then clean and disinfect the wounded area with cotton wool dipped in saline solution (a small amount of salt dissolved in warm water). If such a wound appears to have become infected or otherwise gives you cause for concern, seek veterinary advice.

Abscesses

If an abscess does develop from a wound that has become infected, you will feel it as a throbbing swelling. Because the pus within it needs to be drawn out before the healing process can begin, you can help the process along by pressing a pad of cotton wool soaked in hot (but not boiling) saline solution against the abscess and holding it there for a minute or so before gently drying the abscess, repeating the process four hours later if necessary. When the abscess bursts, wipe away the pus and again disinfect the area with warm saline solution (to which some feline authorities recommend adding a few drops of hydrogen peroxide). If the abscess proves stubbornly resistant to home treatment, take the cat to the vet's – in any case a sensible precaution because antibiotics may be required to prevent reinfection – for the abscess to be lanced. Once clear of pus, the site of the abscess should be kept open for a day or so (and cleaned every few hours) to avoid a new abscess forming.

Insect stings and snake bites

The instinctive response of many cats to flying insects is to try to catch them, which may have painful consequences if the insect in question is a bee or wasp. Unless your cat has been stung in the mouth or on the periphery of the eye, when you should immediately apply an ice cube and then whisk it to the vet's to prevent the ballooning swelling from seriously impeding its breathing or vision, you can treat insect stings yourself. To do this, if it is visible and appears easily removable, pull out the sting with a pair of tweezers and then clean the area with saline solution. The pain of a wasp sting may be alleviated by wiping it with vinegar, and that of a bee sting with a mixture of water and a few drops of hydrogen peroxide. If the sting has broken off, however, which will make its removal difficult, it may be wiser to seek the help of your vet, who may also prescribe an antihistamine ointment.

If you are certain that your cat has been bitten by a snake, but are not sure whether it was of the venomous variety, take it to the vet's at once so that a general anti-venom can be administered before it is too late.

Needles and thread

Lengths of thread exert a magnetic attraction on many felines, which can be particularly dangerous if the thread is attached to a needle. If you think that your cat has swallowed a needle and thread, first open its mouth in the same way as you would to give it a pill (see pages 220 to 221) and check inside to see if the needle has become stuck in its mouth. If you can see the needle, it's best to arrange for the vet to remove it as soon as possible rather than risk damaging the cat (which will no doubt struggle wildly) by trying to extract it yourself. And if you can't see the needle, but still suspect that your cat has ingested it, again take it to the vet's for an X-ray. If your suspicion is confirmed, an operation may be required to extract the needle, which could otherwise cause a serious injury on its passage through the feline digestive system.

If you see a length of thread or string hanging from your cat's rectum, do not attempt to pull it out lest you damage its bowel. If a significant amount of thread is dangling free, cut it to a length of about 5 centimetres (2 inches) so that your cat cannot see it, or get a good hold on it, thereby similarly injuring itself. In most instances, the thread will eventually be excreted through the natural movement of the bowel, but if it is still visible after a few days, consult your vet for further advice.

Burns

IF YOUR CAT HAS A CLOSE ENCOUNTER WITH FIRE, COOL THE BURN WITH COLD WATER OR ICE.

Different types of burn require different emergency treatment, but all will necessitate a follow-up visit to the vet's because the depth – and therefore seriousness – of a burn may not be evident to the inexperienced eye. Scalds or heat burns should be first be cooled either under cold running water or with an ice cube (although some authorities advocate smothering the burn with petroleum jelly, others believe that this simply serves to seal in the heat) and then loosely covered with a piece of cloth, but not bandaged.

Chemical, caustic or acid burns, which may be more widespread, require instant action to remove the corrosive substance from the cat's fur and skin. To do this, fill a bucket, sink or bath with tepid water, add a handful of either sodium bicarbonate (for acid burns) or boracic acid (for caustic burns), don a pair of rubber gloves to protect your own skin and then lift the cat into the water. Be warned, however, that your cat – which will be both frightened and in pain – will struggle, so be firm, but not brutal. Finally, when you think that you have removed all traces of the culprit substance, wrap the cat in a blanket and take it to the veterinary surgery.

Poisoning

PESTICIDES, CERTAIN PAINTS AND A HOST OF OTHER HOUSEHOLD PRODUCTS COULD POISON YOUR CAT.

Rat and mouse poisons contain substances (such as warfarin, arsenic, phosphorus and thallium) that are just as toxic to felines as to rodents, as are many insecticides and other garden pest-control products. Among the more innocuous-seeming household products that may poison your cat can be counted disinfectants (especially those containing phenol), household paint (if it contains lead), creosote, wood preservatives, tar and turpentine. If you intend to use any of these products around your home or garden, it's therefore crucial to keep your cat away from their immediate vicinity. Unfortunately, however, you may not be able to prevent a wandering feline from coming into contact with them in a neighbouring garden.

Although you probably won't have seen your cat ingest a toxin, if it has been poisoned, you'll be alerted to the seriousness of the situation by the dramatic symptoms listed above (see pages 232 to 234), indicating that it requires urgent veterinary treatment if it is to survive, so before you do anything else, phone the vet for advice. If you believe that the cat has been poisoned by licking a toxic substance off its fur, you may be advised to wash it off (see page 242) as soon as you can. And although an emetic – usually in the form of a generous quantity of salt mixed with warm water administered through a plastic syringe (see page 221) – will encourage the cat to vomit up its toxic stomach contents, do not apply this remedy unless your vet has advocated it because regurgitating a corrosive substance could have disastrous consequences for your cat.

DMINISTER SALT AND WATER SOLUTION THROUGH A SYRINGE

Removing toxic substances from a cat's fur

If your cat has clearly had a brush with a freshly creosoted fence or painted wall, do not ignore the evidence in the belief that the feline will simply lick it away itself: not only may this be an insurmountable task, but many such substances will poison your cat if it ingests them through self-grooming. You will therefore have to wash the substances off the feline's fur using a mild shampoo (remember to wear rubber gloves so that your skin remains untainted), followed by a thorough rinsing and drying. Cutting off the affected area of fur may still be necessary. Thereafter, your priority should be a trip to the vet.

Choking and fits

If your cat starts choking (as opposed to preparing to vomit or to expel a furball), and provided that it will allow you to get close enough to examine it, immobilise it by wrapping it in a towel and then open its mouth to see whether its windpipe has been blocked by a foreign object. You may need to depress its tongue with a pencil to get a clear view; shining a torch into its mouth may also help. If there is indeed something in its mouth, reach inside and pull it out with a blunt pair of pliers or tweezers (if you use your fingers, you may be bitten), but if you have no success, you may have to resort to using the emergency procedure recommended for drowning (see page 244). The next step is to take your cat to the vet's immediately.

The sight of a cat having convulsions can be just as frightening for the human spectator as the experience is for the feline suffering the fit, who may be frothing at the mouth and losing control of its bladder and bowels as its body goes into uncontrollable spasms. It's important to keep calm and phone the vet at once for instructions, which you should follow to the letter. You will probably be advised not to approach the cat, but to cover it with a blanket until the fit subsides, whereupon you should wipe away any froth from its mouth and nose to ease its breathing and clean up any accidents. Thereafter, transfer the cat to a dark, quiet and warm place and cover it with a clean blanket until it can receive veterinary attention to ascertain the cause – and poisoning (see pages 240 to 241) is a distinct possibility – that will dictate the treatment.

Electric shock

FORESTALL YOUR CAT RECEIVING AN ELECTRIC SHOCK BY TUCKING ELECTRICAL CABLES OUT OF ITS WAY.

The most common scenario in which felines receive electric shocks is when they chew through an electrical cable. Should this happen to your cat, turn off the power supply before ministering to your stricken feline, whose mouth may still be connected to the cable, but if this is inaccessible, pull on a pair of rubber gloves (in any case a sensible precaution, especially if the shock has caused your cat to release a quantity of electricity-conducting urine) and pull your cat free. The unfortunate cat may have suffered heart failure, so if it appears to be comatose, check its pulse and, if this is weak, try to resuscitate it (see page 246) before ferrying it to the vet's.

Drowning

Should you find your cat lying prone in a puddle or pond, its life is at threat from drowning and you will therefore need to expel the water from its lungs before it succumbs. To do this, first grasp both of its back legs (not its tail) firmly in one hand, raise them so that the cat is upside down and give its back a sharp slap, which should force the water out of its lungs. If that doesn't work, however, the next step is to hold its back legs with one hand and the scruff of its neck with the other and then to swing it firmly downwards. If the situation looks really desperate, and only then, again grasp the cat's back legs and swing it vigorously around in a circle, which should create sufficient centrifugal force for the fluid to be ejected from the lungs through the mouth. Thereafter, you may need to resuscitate the cat by breathing into its nostrils (see page 246).

Broken bones

Even if you don't think that your cat has been involved in a fall or accident, if it is limping badly and the suspect area is swollen, it may have broken a bone. You can test for this by gently lifting the cat onto a table to ascertain whether the suspect leg looks different from its partner or your cat avoids putting any weight onto it. If you think that your cat has sustained a fracture, wrap it gently in a blanket, taking care not to jolt or put pressure on the limb, place it in a large cardboard box and take it to the vet's for an X-ray and whatever further treatment, perhaps a splint, plaster cast or internal pinning, is deemed necessary. Fractures in other parts of the body require urgent veterinary attention.

Stemming bleeding

If your cat is bleeding, but not haemorrhaging, from a wound, you may be able to stem the blood flow by applying a wad of clean fabric (perhaps a handkerchief) or cotton wool to the wound, pressing it down firmly and then bandaging it (see pages 222 to 223).

In cases of profuse bleeding, before applying a pressure bandage, it is usually advisable to try to stem the flow of blood by pressing a wad of cotton wool firmly against the appropriate artery: on the hollow between the neck and shoulder for head and neck wounds; on the bone above the inner elbow (the raised artery should be visible) for the front legs; for the back legs, the corresponding point on the inner thigh; and underneath the base of the tail for tail wounds. Although applying a tourniquet may be effective in halting a haemorrhage, don't attempt this unless you know exactly what you are doing. Thereafter, wash the area with saline solution and apply a pressure bandage. If blood seeps through the bandage, put another over the top, but don't remove the first in case you retard the clotting process.

In both instances, it's important to rush your cat to the vet's as soon as possible because the wound may need stitches and antibiotics.

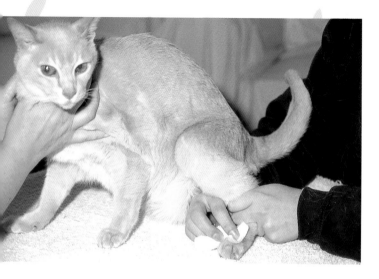

STEM THE FLOW OF BLOOD, THEN BANDAGE

Resuscitating an unconscious cat

Having monitored the unconscious cat's pulse (pages 217 to 218) to ascertain the strength of its vital signs and hence the gravity of its condition, if the situation looks grim, prompt action may save its life. This is especially vital if the feline's eyes are bulging and its gums are turning blue, both of which indicate oxygen deprivation. There are three ways of resuscitating an unconscious cat whose heart may have stopped beating and who has stopped breathing: firstly, by giving it a heart massage to stimulate its heart to resume beating, secondly, by kick-starting the breathing process either by applying pressure to the lungs or, thirdly, by administering mouth-to-nose resuscitation. In all cases, if the cat is wearing one, the first step is to remove its collar to prevent its airways from being restricted, the second being to shift the cat onto its side.

A heart massage can be given by rubbing the flats of both of your hands over the cat's chest, in the process making sure that you apply as little pressure as possible in case you exacerbate any existing damage. With luck, the heart will start to pump blood again, but artificial respiration may nevertheless still be required. Using the flat of one hand, jab it sharply against the cat's chest behind the elbow to encourage air to leave the lungs, then remove your hand for five seconds to enable the lungs to take in air before reapplying the pressure. If this fails to kick-start the breathing process, the next step is to administer mouth-to-nose resuscitation. To do this, first open the cat's mouth and pull out its tongue so that it does not obstruct its windpipe and wipe away any blood, vomit or foreign objects within using a clean cloth. Close the cat's mouth again, tilt back its head slightly, and then, using your lips, blow air into the cat's nostrils for a count of three, take a two-second breather and then repeat the manoeuvre until, it is hoped, your cat shows signs of life.

Whether or not your cat responds positively to these procedures, it will require urgent veterinary treatment (see page 248 for how to transport it as safely as possible to the vet's).

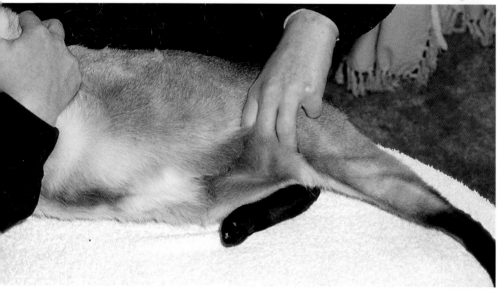

IF YOUR CAT IS UNCONSCIOUS, JUDGE THE GRAVITY OF THE SITUATION BY FIRST TAKING ITS PULSE.

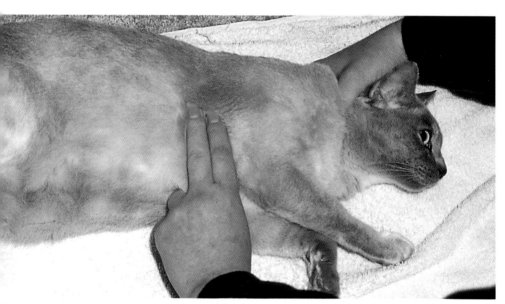

THE NEXT STEP IS TO ASCERTAIN WHETHER THE CAT'S HEART IS STILL BEATING.

Restraining and handling an injured cat

If your cat has had a traumatic or injurious experience, it may have been rendered frantic with shock and pain, in which case you will have to restrain it, both so that you can examine it and to prepare it for transportation to the veterinary surgery. One way of doing this is to encircle the upright cat's chest with one hand and, with the other, to grip the scruff of its neck firmly, which should trigger a kittenhood reflex that makes it freeze, enabling you to pick it up (not by its scruff, but by supporting its chest and nether regions) and wrap it in a blanket before transferring it to a cat-carrier or cardboard box. In more extreme circumstances, you may have to chase the panic-stricken cat into a room, shut the door and throw a towel or blanket over it so that you can pick it up without sustaining painful lacerations from its teeth and claws (putting on a pair of thick gardening gloves may literally save your skin). Try to calm the feline down during the immobilisation process by talking to it quietly and comfortingly.

If the injured cat is already immobile – perhaps following a fall or traffic accident – it's generally not advisable to alter the position in which it is lying lest you inflict additional damage on the cat's body. That having been said, however, the best way to prepare it for transportation, and lessen the risk of injuring it further, is gently to shift it onto its side. As delicately as you can, and with your palms facing upward, place one hand under its chest, where the front legs meet the torso, and the other under its pelvis, where the back legs adjoin its body. (Never, however, lift up its head in case you cause it to choke on blood or vomit, although if you can arrange its head so that it is a little lower than its body while still being supported, this will ward off brain damage.) Thereafter, first lift it onto a blanket or towel and, preferably with you holding one end of the blanket or towel and someone else the other to minimise any jolting, transfer the makeshift stretcher into a large cardboard box (or a cat-carrier, although a box may be more secure). Cover the cat with another blanket to keep it warm – and, if possible, place a warm hot-water bottle near it – to prevent it from going into deeper shock, before taking it to the veterinary surgery, doing your best to make the transportation process as smooth as possible to avoid aggravating the cat's injuries.

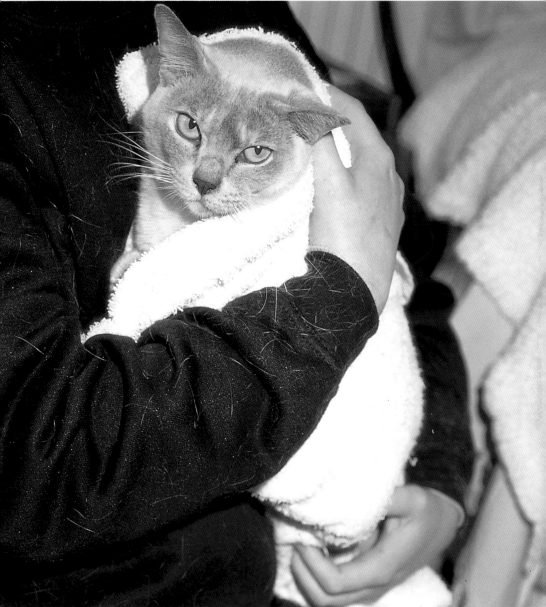

IMMOBILISE A PANIC-STRICKEN CAT BY WRAPPING IT IN A TOWEL.

INDEX

 **index**

H

handling 130–2

    an injured cat 248

    by children 132

harvest mites 200

haw problems 210

health 96–7. 216–18

history and origins 9–18

housetraining 84, 178–182

hunting 30, 34, 36–41, 45

hygiene 167–8

I

immune system 141–2

insect stings 237

K

kittens 59, 61, 83–4, 86, 88, 96–7, 98

    caring for 160–3

    development 163

    feeding 163

    giving birth to 156–160

L

lice 199

litter 81, 108–9

    hygiene 168

lumps and bumps 232

M

maggots 200–1

mange mites 199–200

medication 219, 220–1

mobility problems 232

mouth 50, 51

    afflictions of 213–15

    taste 53–4

moving house 186, 188

N

neutering 59, 86, 155

nose 50, 97

    afflictions of 212–13

    smell 54, 55–7, 58

nursing 143, 224–6

P

personality 90–2, 98

Bibliography

Allan, Eric; Bonning, Lynda; and Blogg, J Rowan, *Everycat*, Methuen Australia Pty Ltd, 1985.

Bradshaw, Dr John, *The true nature of the cat*, Boxtree Limited, London, 1993.

Carr, Samuel (ed), *The poetry of cats*, Chancellor Press, London, 1986.

Chevalier, Jean, and Gheerbrant, Alain, *The Penguin dictionary of symbols*, Penguin Books, London, 1996.

Cooper, J C, *An illustrated encyclopaedia of traditional symbols*, Thames and Hudson Ltd, London, 1993.

Cutts, Paddy, *Cat breeds of the world*, Anness Publishing Ltd, London, 1993.

Cutts, Paddy, *The cat care manual*, Anness Publishing Ltd, London, 1999.

Fontana, David, *The secret language of symbols*, Pavilion Books Ltd, London, 1993.

Gibson, Clare, *Signs and symbols*, Grange Books plc, London, 1996.

Goss, Wendy, *Looking after your cat*, Hamlyn Publishing Group Ltd, London, 1990.

Hall, James, *Hall's illustrated dictionary of symbols in Eastern and Western art*, John Murray, London, 1994.

Julien, Nadia, *The mammoth dictionary of symbols*, Robinson Publishing, London, 1996.

Moore, Joan, *The cat lover's companion*, Colour Library Books, Godalming, 1992.

Morris, Desmond, *Catwatching and catlore*, Arrow Books Ltd, London, 1992.

O'Neill, Amanda, *The best-ever book of cats*, Larousse plc, London, 1998.

Pirinçci, Akif and Degen, Rolf, *Cat sense*, Fourth Estate, London, 1994.

Pond, Grace, *Purnell's pictorial encyclopedia of cats*, Purnell Books, Maidenhead, 1980.

Richter, Jack, *Your talking cat*, The Promotion Department, Inc, USA, 1991.

Loxton, Howard, *Cats*, Collins, London and Glasgow, 1985.

Loxton, Howard, *Guide to the cats of the world*, Treasure Press, London, 1990.

Taylor, David, *You and your cat*, Doring Kindersley Ltd, London, 1986.

Manolson, Frank, *Understanding your cat*, Quarto Publishing plc, London, 1989.

Walker, Barbara G, *The woman's dictionary of symbols and sacred objects*, Pandora, London, 1988.

McHattie, Grace, *Kitten care for children*, André Deutsch Ltd, London, 1989.

Dedication, credits and acknowledgements

Clare Gibson dedicates this book to Alice and Olivia Malan de Mérindol and also extends her appreciative thanks to Mike Haworth–Maden, John Gibson and Marianne Gibson for their help and support.

Acknowledgements

Photographic Coordinator - Nicky Juneman
Assistant - Ena Tulloch
Veterinary Surgery - McFarlane & Associates

Picture Credits

Pictures pp9, 14, 24,133br © Photodisk

(where b = bottom and r = right)

Introduction

introduction

I, born of a race of strange things,
Of deserts, great temples, great kings,
In the hot sands where the nightingale never sings!
Ford Madox Ford, from *The cat of the house*.

ALL CATS HAVE ANCIENT EGYPTIAN ANCESTRY.

The ambivalence with which it is regarded has elevated the cat to a unique position among domestic animals. Since it first chose to co-exist with humans around four millennia ago, the cat has appeared as a home-loving creature of comfort by day that transforms itself into a wild hunter by night. An enigmatic character, it has become an object of admiration and worship on the one hand, and a victim of suspicion and persecution on the other. Perhaps the key to unlocking the paradox of the cat is that it made a pragmatic choice to throw in its lot with humankind, without ever forfeiting the streak of wildness that earns it the respect of those who appreciate its independent character and the vilification of those who are unsettled by its inscrutability. And, as Ford Madox Brown observed, every cat of the house, be it a humble moggie or pampered pedigree, exudes an air of exotic mystery, its cool, self-contained gaze taking us back in time to the 'hot sands' and 'strange things' of its ancient Egyptian ancestors.

Out of Africa

The domestic cat, *Felis catus* or *Felis domesticus*, can trace its lineage back 50 million years, to the *Miacis* from which the *Dinictis*, *Machairodus* and eventually today's cat family, the *Felidae* (which comprises *Acinonyx*, cheetahs; *Panthera*, big cats; and *Felis*, small cats), evolved. And although the specific ancestry of the domestic cat has been veiled by the mists of time, and further clouded by the interbreeding of various species of wildcat the world over, genetic analysis indicates that most

European domestic cats are descended from the African wildcat, *Felis sylvestris lybica*.

The history of the African wildcat's domestication is depicted in ancient Egyptian art, the world's earliest feline image being seen in an Egyptian tomb painting dating from around 2600 BC. Although the subject of this portrait is probably an African wildcat, the house cats that are immortalised in the tomb paintings found at Dier el Medina show that by 1600 BC certain members of the *Felis sylvestris*

IT WAS THE ANCIENT EGYPTIANS WHO FIRST DOMESTICATED THE CAT.

9

lybica family had become domesticated. The most likely reason why these cats initially consented to exchange their wildcat lifestyle for one of domestication – and why the ancient Egyptians welcomed them into their homes – is that of mutual benefit, the cats finding plentiful prey around the Egyptians' grain stores and the Egyptians in turn valuing their efficiency as pest-controllers. A practical relationship of mutual advantage was established, and cats eventually came to be prized as far more than just skilled mousers and keen-eyed killers of the snakes that slithered into Egyptian homes.

Cats feature largely in the mythology of ancient Egypt, and always as protectors: the cat-headed goddess Mafdet, for example, being venerated for her role in protecting the pharaoh's palace from venomous snakes. The goddess who was primarily responsible for elevating the cat to its sacred status, however, was Bast, or Bastet, the cat-headed sister of Sekhmet (the lion-headed war goddess) and either the wife or sister of Ra (the Egyptians' sun god and supreme deity), who slayed the underworld serpent Apep before it could capsize the boat in which Ra traversed the sky by day. Worshipped as the vigilant guardian of the sun god, as well as the home, Bast was especially revered as a moon goddess

who had the power to bestow the gift of fertility upon her worshippers. Along with their snake-killing prowess, another reason why cats were so closely identified with Bast can be seen in their waxing and waning pupils, for, as Edward Topsell reported in 1607, in his *Historie of Foure-footed Beasts*,

The Egyptians have observed in the eyes of a Cat, the encrease of the Moonlight for with the Moone, they shine more fully at the full, and more dimly in the change and wain, and the male Cat doth also vary his eyes with the Sunne; for when the Sunne ariseth, the apple of his eye is long; towards noone it is round, and at the evening it cannot be seene at all, but the whole eye sheweth alike.

While female cats were associated with the moon goddess, and toms with the sun god, all cats were sacred to Bast, the 'mother' of cats whose centre of worship was the city of Bubastis. Cats led a pampered existence at Bast's temple in Bubastis, being embalmed and mummified when they died before being interned in a vast feline necropolis. It was certainly a cat's life in Egypt, particularly after Bast became the national deity in around 950 BC. The Greek historian Herodotus, writing in about 450 BC, tells us that when a house cat died, the whole family shaved off their eyebrows as a sign of mourning, Diodorus Siculus adding during the first century BC that killing a cat was a crime punishable by death.

Cats were jealously guarded against abduction from Egypt by unworthy foreigners (although a few were probably smuggled out by Phoenician traders), but things changed when the rule of the pharaoh was replaced by that of the Roman emperor in 30 BC. By AD 390 Bast's worship had been banned, and with Egypt's star in decline and Rome's in the ascendant, some of the deposed goddess's sacred creatures travelled to the outposts of the Roman Empire with the legions (who, no doubt, valued their rodent-killing services aboard their galley ships), others following the Silk Road to the Far East.

Although they were never venerated to the exalted degree enjoyed by the sacred cats of Egypt, their Graeco-Roman descendants were nevertheless accorded respect through their association with the Greek moon goddess Artemis and her Roman counterpart Diana, both of whom were equated with Bast. And with the spreading of the Graeco-Roman influence throughout Europe, cats were said to pull the vehicle of Freya, the goddess of fertility whose appearance in Norse mythology may have been inspired by the prototypical figure of Cybele, the fierce Phrygian mother goddess who travelled in a lion-drawn chariot (the feline discrepancy being due to the prevalence of wildcats, and not lions, throughout Northern Europe). And if

LIONS WERE SAID TO PULL CYBELE'S CHARIOT, AND SMALLER EUROPEAN WILDCATS THAT OF FREYA.

11

introduction

their religious associations won them some honour, their vermin-suppressing prowess covered them with glory, cats forcing the mongoose, ferret and stone marten to concede their combined title of Rome's champion rat-killers during the fourth century AD. Wherever they lived, cats were highly valued for their hunting skills, as was reflected by a decree made in 948 by the Welsh prince Howel the Good, that anyone who killed or stole one of his granary's cats would be made to forfeit

a sheep, lamb or a considerable quantity of grain.

Cats of the Orient

At the same time as cats were hard at work controlling European rodents, their Oriental brethren were providing a similar service in the paddy fields and silk farms of China and Japan. In the Far East, however, cats were as much admired for their sleek feline beauty as for their hunting skills. The *Cat Book Poems* of medieval

THE SMOOTH FUR AND SLEEK APPEARANCE OF CATS WAS HIGHLY VALUED IN THE FAR EAST.

Siam (Thailand), for example, praised the Korat for its 'hairs so smooth, with tips like clouds and roots like silver, with eyes that shine like dewdrops on a lotus leaf'. In contrast to Europe's workaday felines, the ancestors of such sacred cats as the Korat, Siamese and Burmese were cherished for their elegant appearance and were therefore prevented from crossbreeding, with the result that most Oriental purebreds have unbroken pedigrees that stretch back for centuries.

There are many stories attached to Oriental cats, some connected to their physical characteristics and others explaining why they are worthy of honour. In the Buddhist belief of Thailand, for example, when an extremely rarefied human spirit dies, their soul enters a Siamese cat and only attains nirvana when the cat in turn passes away. Indeed, during the twentieth century, it was still the custom for a Siamese cat, into which, it was believed, the recently deceased king of Siam's soul had passed, to attend the coronation of his successor. Another tale speaks of how the Birman, Burma's sacred cat, gained its golden fur and blue eyes when a priest of the Khmer temple at Lao-Tsun died while invoking the aid of the goddess Tsun-Kyan-Kse to repel a

Siamese raid on her temple, his prayers being answered after his spirit left his body and entered his favourite cat, who also assumed the goddess's colouring.

Other Oriental beliefs concerning cats are, however, less complimentary, it being said, for instance, that the cat is cursed because it did not mourn the death of Buddha. And Chinese and Japanese folk belief swings from regarding the cat as a bringer of prosperity (probably because it is the enemy of destructive rodents) to fearing it as a malevolent shape-shifter that heralds misfortune. Although the Maneki-Neko, the effigy of a cat that beckons with its left paw, is a symbol of good luck in Japan that is kept in many homes, many felines are thought to be the bringers of death and destruction. Considered a *yin* creature of the night in China, white cats are said to be turned into demons by the moon's rays, while in Japan, a race of vampire cats (whose forked tails fortunately make them instantly recognisable) are furthermore said to murder women, take on their appearance and, thus disguised, suck the life-blood out of their sleeping bedfellows. Similarly, cases of cot death in Europe were once blamed on vampire cats that allegedly fed on the breath of babies.

13

CATS ARE REGARDED WITH AFFECTION IN ISLAMIC TRADITION.

Feline superstitions

Despite such Far Eastern reservations about the cat's exact intentions towards humanity, it is considered wise to hedge one's bets and to treat cats with respect, as in Persia (Iran), where black cats are said to be jinns (spirits that assume feline form) or hemzads (individuals' guardian 'angels'). The world over, the cat's mysterious, far-seeing eyes are considered to reveal its clairvoyant powers, as well as its agility and cunning ingenuity, just some of the characteristics for which it is respected as a totemic animal by many African and Native American peoples.

Two charming stories from Islamic tradition reveal why the cat is regarded with affection by many Muslims. The first tells that when a pair of rats multiplied and over-ran Noah's ark, Noah stroked the lion's nose, its reflexive sneeze producing two cats who swiftly solved Noah's vermin problem. The second relates that the 'M' that can be seen on many cats' foreheads is the mark that was made by the Prophet Mohammed when he stroked his favourite cat. Interestingly, this explanation for the cat's 'M' has a parallel in a long-forgotten Christian tradition, it being said that it is evidence of the Virgin Mary's